"Shaping True Story into Screenplay turns the basics of screenwriting toward the task of telling one's true story." – Mitchell Levin, Senior Story Analyst, DreamWorks

"Having relied on Candace's instincts, judgment, and clarity, I can testify that she is the absolute best, and consider Shaping True Story into Screenplay a great gift. So will anyone who reads it." - *Robert Palmer (Manager of Anthony Hopkins, Faye Dunaway, and Dick Van Dyke)*

"Candace Kearns Read is an extremely talented screenwriter and story analyst. Anyone intending to develop material based on 'real life' will benefit from the wisdom and experience found within these pages." - *Ben Press (Founding Partner, Fortitude Talent Agency)*

"Candace Kearns Read has a knack for whipping a weak script into shape. She is tough, but in the kindest way. This book will be an invaluable resource to all writers and directors." - *Jeff Woolnough (Director,* OUTER LIMITS, THE DON CHERRY STORY *and* CELINE*)*

"Candace is a highly regarded script analyst and writer. In this book, Candace impeccably shares her great skill and creativity to help screenwriters, and expertly enables you to develop your greatest possession into a compelling screenplay, by guiding you to write what you know best: Yourself." - *Tony Greco, Screenwriters Online*

Shaping True Story

into Screenplay

by

Candace Kearns Read

Acknowledgements

This book would not have been written without the persistence and encouragement of Paula Press, who has championed true story screenwriting like nobody's business. I would also like to thank my agent, Sandra Bond, and my manager, Daniel Corrieri. Many thanks to Cara Lopez Lee for all of her help during the proposal phase. I am grateful to Amy Johnson and Lesley Kenney for all of their efforts to get the word out, and also wish to thank Bob Palmer, Ben Press, Jeff Woolnough, Bret Carr, and Donzaleigh Abernathy for their encouragement and support of this book.

I have had many generous mentors along the way, and they include New York University's Mark Dickerman, Karen Malpede and D.B. Gilles, Antioch University's Hope Edelman, David Ulin, Paul Lisicky, Tara Ison and Eloise Klein Healy. I find ongoing support from The Girdles: Rebecca Kuder, Elaine Gale, Julia Kress Herrington, Chris Benda, Kerri Valentino, Saroya Habeych, Lisa Brooks and Vanja Thompson. My deep appreciation goes out to NYU's Dramatic Writing Program and Antioch Los Angeles' Master of Fine Arts in Creative Writing, as well as Denver's Lighthouse Writers Workshop, with special thanks to Shari Caudron. Gratitude beyond words goes out to my husband, Mike Read, for his enduring support.

TABLE OF CONTENTS

Introduction:

In Praise of Navel Gazing

When I tell people I'm a story analyst in the film industry, they almost always say something like, "I have a story that would make a great movie." And the funny thing is, they usually do have a great story. It seems that almost everyone has lived through or experienced something dramatic, interesting, and memorable. It also seems that quite a few people would like to share their story with others through the medium of film.

Why do we seek to immortalize ourselves in stories, and envision our lives on the big screen? Is it pure narcissism, nothing more than self-indulgent navel gazing? Or is it because we have something to say, something to share with others, and a desire to teach and help people by allowing them to learn from our experience? In the best of all scenarios, it is out of a sense of purpose, to heal ourselves and others, but also to share and connect with others. We seek meaning from our experiences, and we try to make sense of who we are and the cards we've been dealt in life.

As humans, we instinctually and intuitively need to make sense of things. By taking the painful, shocking and disturbing, the miraculous, beautiful and touching, and telling our stories, we re-see them, put things in perspective and tame the wild beast that is unpredictable, mysterious life. When we transform our experiences into a story with a beginning, middle and end, protagonist and antagonist, rising arc, plot turns and a resolution, then suddenly we can see what it is we needed to learn. So, yes, it is cathartic to write a screenplay based on our own experience, and yes, it does require that we take some time to think about ourselves. We reminisce, remember and re-frame. We infuse our memories with imaginative touches. And sometimes we even fill in the blanks with fictionalized material, because who can remember it all exactly the way it happened?

We may be dwelling on ourselves, wallowing even, for a while, but this is not a selfish act. It is a generous one, designed to lift others' consciousness, even as we rise above our own pain and resentments to find the philosophical truths, the core, and the message. The process of autobiographical and biographical screenwriting demands that we break it down, take things we've done and things that have happened to us (or people we know) and create an adventure out of them. We turn our memories into journeys, and even though ours is just one out of millions of journeys taken in this world by millions of people, it is one of value. It is one whose truths about the human condition can be captured in the visual medium, made poetic with imagery that transports, and spoken out through dialogue that evokes the essence of who we are: unique and individual, yet still universal and transcendent.

Screenwriting guru Robert McKee tells us in his weighty and profound book *Story: Substance, Structure, Style and the Principles of Screenwriting* that "Fact, no matter how minutely observed, is truth with a small "t." Big "T" truth is located behind, beyond, inside, below the surface of things…and cannot be directly observed." The impulse to write from our lives comes easily, but the completion of a marketable screenplay is another thing altogether. The leap to big T truth requires artful, imaginative reshaping.

Many of the worlds' greatest dramas have been based on true stories, whether biographies or autobiographies – from the early days of CITIZEN KANE, BATTLESHIP POTEMKIN and PATTON to the later part of the 20th Century with MISSISSIPPI BURNING, GOODFELLAS, GLORY, MY LEFT FOOT, DINER, and OUT OF AFRICA, and more recently, *21*, THE BLIND SIDE, INVICTUS, SEABISCUIT, 127 HOURS and THE SOCIAL NETWORK, to name just a few.

How do you take the raw material of a life, be it your own or someone else's, and shape it into an engaging, cinematic screen story? The answer is not simple or straightforward. Huge leaps of imagination must be taken. New perspectives must be found. Events and characters must be truncated and condensed, combined and enhanced for dramatic effect.

In some sense, all stories are autobiographical. Every writer, no matter how much they think they're telling a wildly imaginative, completely invented story, is actually writing about themselves, exploring issues from their psyche, and drawing upon memories of their lives.

But this book is designed for those of you who want to tell your own true story, or that of someone else. Rather than thinking you're making up a story but are actually telling a true one, you will be thinking you're telling a true story when actually, you're making it up. This is because all experience, in order to be retold, must be reframed, reinvented, re-seen and revised through the lens of your unique perspective.

Lost in the woods of your memories and research, alone with a mass of experience and issues, with no clear criteria for what should belong in the screenplay and what should not, the work of getting your life story down can be overwhelming. With frequent stops and starts, and as E.B. White describes, "steering by stars which are disturbingly in motion," the process can be torturous and frustrating, ultimately ending in despair. This book is designed to make it a pleasurable, life-affirming experience, full of self-discovery, epiphanies and breakthroughs, culminating in the completion of an engrossing and marketable script.

Part practical guidebook and part inspirational tool, this book is here to encourage you to find metaphors for truer expression, stimulate your imagination, and help you visualize solutions to your screenwriting problems as it explains how to:

- Clarify the themes of your true story and use them as a springboard for the development of plot and character
- Shape the plot into a personalized three-act structure along a focused spine
- Layer the story with complementary, cohesive subplots
- Build character arcs from the motivations and conflicts in real life
- Invent a frame to propel the story forward
- Imagine events to create scenes that are metaphors for real events
- Choose what to leave out in the interest of story

If telling a great story is your goal, then you've come to the right place. The purpose of this book is to help you transform the raw materials of your memories (or research into someone else's life) into a great movie script. What you will discover will surprise you, because you will be taking a journey of personal exploration as you write.

This book will break what might seem like a gargantuan process down into bite-sized pieces, and give you short, easy writing exercises so you won't even realize you're writing the script when you actually are.

The first step is to leave reality behind and enter the world of story. Trust me, your memories will follow you there. But keep your eyes on the prize: a script the reader can't put down, with tension, conflict, humor, poignancy, unforgettable characters, and a meaningful theme that resonates with universal appeal.

This will take time. Some amount of neglect and abandonment of reality will be required. You will have to leave what really happened by the wayside and dream up metaphors for truth instead. And you may have some bad hair days, because you'll be too busy living in your story to take a shower. But if you stay true to the instinct, and do justice to the story within that is yearning to be told, the rewards will be great.

Chapter One:

Sculpting Screen Story from the Clay of Life

Do you have an idea from your own life experience or that of someone else's that you think would make a great movie? Great! But where do you start? Do you rush out and buy some software and then just write down everything that comes to mind? Do you meticulously plan it out into a three-act structure, and then stare at the outline, waiting for inspiration? Do you just keep thinking about it and hope that someday it will be clear enough in your mind to write itself? As you've probably guessed, none of these approaches are likely to produce a well-crafted, engaging screenplay.

What's missing in many people's approach to writing a script based on their own life experience or that of someone else's is an organic, intuitive element to the process. This involves clarifying a journey, identifying its themes, and creating a relevant metaphor as we structure a plot and develop characters to contain and shape the nebulous clay that is "real life."

It's hard to know where to start. It's hard to know how to proceed. Even if you have a clear idea of what you're doing, it's easy to get lost along the way. How can you be objective when you're writing about yourself, or someone you know well, either through experience or research? How can you avoid narcissism and self-indulgent writing? Somehow, we need to move beyond pure self-expression, dumping, venting, and mere reminiscing. Somehow, we need to rise above and tell a great story.

The process starts with articulating the theme, or moral, of the story only you can tell. It's time to find the meaning, and the reason you are driven to tell this story. What lesson does it offer? Once you have that in mind, you can playfully explore within the realm of imagination, and find the metaphor that will serve as a springboard for the development of plot and character. From there, you need only be willing to allow those characters and plot to grow together. In the process, you will notice that character and plot are not two separate things, but are actually interdependent. One informs the other, which in turn informs the first, and around and around it goes, in a relationship that is more circular than linear.

What is truth? Is truth what actually happened, according to your perspective, or is truth the emotional resonance, the meaning inferred, and the indescribable essence of something? Truth captures perfectly how an event or situation affected you, filled with all the nuance and subtleties of... real life. When we create metaphors using story, we make the personal universal by tapping into the collective unconscious.

Focusing on metaphor works beautifully for screen story development because film is in many ways quite similar to poetry. In each, imagery is of prime importance. In each, an organic rhythm and pace must be felt. And in each, brevity is the key and less is usually more.

The truth is, you can't ever tell the story of a life in a film. But you can use autobiographical or biographical material to create a metaphor for the emotional journey you or another person has taken. And the best part of this is that often, a metaphor can express the truth much more clearly and effectively than a factual retelling.

You may be thinking that this all makes sense, but wondering how in the world you can make it happen. Well, the strange and wonderful thing about this process is that you don't need to make it happen. That's because, in a way, it has already happened, by virtue of the fact that you have already lived through your story. You have experienced it, or if it's the story of someone else's life you're writing about, then you've researched it well enough to have experienced it vicariously. Somewhere deep in your subconscious, you have internalized the story, and somewhere deep down in your brain, you've already begun to make sense of it.

What I'm suggesting is that in your subconscious, the metaphor already exists. All of the themes of your story, and the multitude of ways those themes can be expressed, are already in the back of your mind, ripe for the picking. This makes your work much easier, and your path much clearer. All you have to do is open your mind and allow this story to come forth.

Think about it. You know your story. You've lived it, or read all about it. You've thought about it, felt the feelings and decided there's something there – something important enough to share with others. It's exciting and visual enough for the big or small screen. You already hold in your mind all the keys to writing a great screenplay based on your experience, or that of someone close to you.

And yet, it's overwhelming, and tough to know exactly what to put in, how to arrange it, and how to fit it into a dramatic shape. What is the arc? You're not quite sure. Where is the climax? How does it start? And how does it all resolve? Some of these essential craft questions are probably still lurking unanswered in your mind.

Sometimes it feels like a tough mountain to climb, and in fact, it is. But, just as with a mountain, there are treasures lying deep within. You won't get to the heart of your story, or to the core of your personal truth, by staying on the surface, running up and down the mountain, arguing and explaining, describing and recounting. Instead, you're going to quietly dig inside, by asking yourself to articulate the meaning first. Let's get clear on the theme of your story, and find the nugget that is your personal growth.

Even if this is someone else's story, it is still about you and your journey. Otherwise, you wouldn't have been drawn to it. You might even think of yourself as having been chosen by this story. In any event, it is your passion now to explore the world of these issues and events, these characters, situations and themes. Someone else may have had the experiences you want to write about. But your passion for telling their story indicates that you identify with their journey so strongly that you may as well have taken it yourself.

Ask yourself, what is the lesson learned as a result of having lived through the experiences you're writing about? This is what will make your story worth telling, and it will be your screenplay's raison d'etre. This is also what will help you mine the memories and find the gold.

Fortunately, you don't have to stumble around in the dark,

pouring out your story on the page using reams and reams of paper as you recall scenes and situations and then try to shape it all into something with a beginning, middle and end. Instead, there is a method you can follow, a path which leads from the abstract to the concrete.

The method is not a cure-all, and it will need to be adapted to suit each individual writer, but in general it looks like this:

1. Articulate the theme of the journey taken

2. Develop a metaphor within the context of story that will evoke that theme

3. Design a character arc, a story of personal growth, and an inner journey that exemplifies that theme and manifests it into events and scenes

4. Hone and shape a storyline to take the characters on that journey, making it fit into the schema of a three act structure

5. Use invention and imagination for the development of "fictional" scenes and a framing device

6. Use memory and specificity to further develop the character traits, scene descriptions, actions and dialogue

7. Put it all together in a draft, then revise to your heart and soul's content

You have probably noticed an emphasis on theme in this approach. There are several reasons for this. Theme helps you keep the story focused, and enables you to choose which scenes to keep and which to leave out. It makes the script more entertaining, by conveying some valuable lesson or nugget of meaning, which audiences always find satisfying, as long as the theme is not presented too obviously.

One of the most exciting things about identifying your theme is that it can help you define and create a quest for the main character to embark upon. This then outlines and projects the main character's journey, which in turn, suggests a storyline.

First, you have to attain some distance from the facts, in order to invent a new storyline that can serve as a metaphor for what really happened. What ends up in the screenplay, if it is to be viable as a film, is not an exact replay of your true story, but a dramatization that captures the essence of what really happened.

Translating your true story into screenplay requires a combination of memory and imagination. The idea is to detach yourself from what really happened in order to mold your truth into an entertaining storyline.

Try This!

Write two pages of beginning, middle and end. What happened? What happened next? Then what happened? Sometimes the end becomes the beginning and vice versa, but try to write, in small vignettes, anecdotes, and scenes from memory or research, a summary of the beginning, middle and end of your story. You may end up with two pages or ten. Just keep writing until you've told the whole thing.

Now, write about the themes of this story. What's to be learned here? What's the moral of the story? What is story trying to say? (Hint: Think about what your characters learn in the course of the story — these lessons are your story's themes and morals.) There's no one right answer. Brainstorm several different possibilities until you find the most powerful theme.

CHAPTER 2:

Finding the Metaphor of Your Personal Journey

When we have a true story that seems worth telling, usually it is because we have taken a personal journey. We've gone through something, come out the other side, and gained some nugget of wisdom about life. Perhaps it wasn't us that took this journey, but someone we know or have read about. Their journey inspires us to such a degree that we feel compelled to tell their story in the form of a screenplay. The important thing is that from this personal journey of growth, a metaphor can be found, and used to show others a glimpse of our truth.

First, we need to differentiate between the "facts" of what happened, and the "truth" about how those events and situations affected those involved, and changed people's lives and their thinking. Whether this life experience was a relationship drama, an action-adventure, a comic situation, or some combination of the above, we need to think about what the feelings were along the way, how the people involved (ourselves or others) grew and changed, and what was ultimately learned.

The journey is always one of growth and enlightenment; otherwise it wouldn't be worth writing about or seeing up on the screen. We are sense-making creatures, and story is a sense-making

9

vehicle. Through film, we try to make sense of our experiences, and in the process, we discover the seeds of a good story.

The author Orson Scott Card once said that "Metaphors have a way of holding the most truth in the least space." What is a metaphor? It is the use of imagery or symbolism to represent something. An abstract idea or feeling, a theme, is given concrete body and finds a home in one tangible thing. In CITIZEN KANE it was a sled named Rosebud. In ON GOLDEN POND it was a trout named Walter. This concrete, sensory embodiment is necessary in the medium of film. A good screenplay is not made up of ideas, themes or feelings. Instead it is made up of concrete, sensory visuals, and it is filled with action and images.

Think about some films based on true stories. Examples of metaphors used well include RUNNING WITH SCISSORS (the scissors represent cutting off manhood), BORN ON THE 4TH OF JULY (Fireworks representing the violence and glory of our country), DINER (the setting of the diner as an emblem for community), ANGELA'S ASHES (the ashes representing the inability to nurture), and MY LEFT FOOT (his foot a symbol for using what we've been given.) In all of the above examples, the metaphor is a concrete object, something that can be seen and/or heard, held or touched. It is something that has sensory power and can be easily portrayed on film. But the deeper, more compelling reason we look to metaphor when developing our own life story into film is that metaphor often expresses the big "T" Truth much more effectively than a factual re-telling.

Once you find your metaphor, it will shed light on the

alchemic process of shaping true story into screenplay. So take the time to think about your metaphor. Live with the possibilities for a while, and see what you can dream up.

In AMELIA, written by Ron Bass and Anna Hamilton Phelan, the writers did a great job of evoking the themes of her life through the visual metaphor of flying. Flying became a metaphor for the freedom she sought and found, both in life and death. Independent to a fault, Amelia Earhart fiercely eschewed the constraints of marriage, monogamy, and marketing, just to name a few, in her headstrong drive to maintain her freedom. In the film, Amelia, portrayed by Hillary Swank, agrees to do commercials to raise funds for her flights, but refuses to be a puppet in her endorsements. She finally agrees to marry Putnam, but then has an affair with Vidal. When Vidal wants to keep her too close, she resigns and goes back to her husband, who, as it turns out, was as willing to support her freedom as anyone could ever be.

In voice over narration taken from Earhart's real writings, Swank as Amelia conveys the sense of transcendence she feels when clouds meet the sea: "Everyone has oceans to fly. As long as you have the heart to do it. Is it reckless? Maybe. But what do dreams know of boundaries?" We hear these words against the visual backdrop of her flying the plane over vast stretches of ocean.

In order to make meaning, often the subject of the film becomes a metaphor for something else, as in THE PIANIST (the piano as a symbol of the supremacy of art over war), and HOTEL RWANDA (the hotel as a symbol of shelter for valuable human lives.) These films highlight an individual of extraordinary achievement or determination, and the central character becomes a metaphor for this singular focus and dedication, and for their spirit.

To understand metaphor, think about levels of meaning, and how one thing can represent several different things at once. For example, AWAKENINGS is not just about catatonic patients being roused into consciousness, it is also about the awakening of a doctor to his own life.

Here are some other films with a central metaphor that helps reveal the theme and give direction to the story line. As is often the case, the title contains the imagery of the central metaphor and thus helps convey the theme clearly without it having to be stated in the dialogue or some other obvious, heavy-handed way in the film itself.

MONSTER – This title and image raises the question of whether Aileen, one of the first female serial killers in history, was a monster or not. In Roger Ebert's review, January of 2004, he says, "Her image on the news and in documentaries presented a large, beaten-down woman who did seem to be monstrous," and he then goes on to imply that the film and Charlize Theron's portrayal of her contradict that notion and attempt to humanize her.

WALK THE LINE – The title is taken from a song by Johnny Cash, and refers to the singers' ability to obey the rules, to conform in spite of his nature, for the sake of his love for June Carter. In this case, the image of walking a line serves to represent the abstract idea of conformity, staying on the straight and narrow. And in the film, the metaphor serves as a basis for the idea that although it is not in Cash's nature to conform, his love for June is so strong that he wants to overcome his inner weaknesses.

SEABISQUIT – The title refers to a horse who became an unexpected hero during the Depression, when everyone needed something to lift their spirits. A seabisquit is a small, hard, cracker that was used on ships and as army rations years ago. We are given a metaphor then, for something small and rough that will endure hardship, which is exactly what many feel the horse did.

MY LEFT FOOT – Refers to the only limb that Christy Brown, author of the memoir on which the film was based, could use, because of the cerebral palsy he was born with. The fact that he uses his left foot to become a successful writer and painter expresses the idea of overcoming adversity through sheer determination.

Aside from metaphor, films have other things in common with poetry. They both need to be concise and rhythmic, and both use subtext and imagery to express their ideas. As an exercise, go to your local bookstore and browse the poetry section. Try to find a book of poetry that speaks to you, that resonates with subject matter you can relate to. Take the book home and set it by your bedside to read each night. Let it be the last thing you think of before drifting off to sleep. Keep a pad and pen by your bed and try to make some notes about your script first thing in the morning. Notice how the act of reading and appreciating poetry can inspire your own ability to infuse your work with metaphor and imagery.

In a poem, the medium for expression is imagery. Words on the page paint pictures. And of course, the same is true for the extremely visual medium of film. What is imagery? It is not just pictures for their own sake, but pictures with depth, layers and hidden meanings. Like the loaded question that a lawyer asks to provoke the jury towards deeper thought, the well-chosen filmic image conveys more than words could ever get across.

Every time you find a concrete visual image to describe while writing your script, you're giving us imagery. But sometimes, that picture you're painting will represent something profound, something words cannot capture, such as a lone trekker on a barren arctic glacier, or a middle-aged woman dining by herself on the beach. These images hit us in a visceral place, going straight to the gut, and because they take us out of our rational minds and into the emotional realm, we are affected deeply, and what we see on the screen becomes embedded in our memory forever.

What do you remember from your favorite films? Is it the dialogue? Or is it the images that your mind and heart retain? The runners on the beach in CHARIOTS OF FIRE? ROCKY on the steps? PATCH ADAMS wearing a clown nose while he treats a dying little girl? As you craft your script, search your imagination for the images that will best express what words cannot.

Another way to incorporate poetic technique in your screenwriting without seeming overly poetic is to use subtext in your dialogue. All of your character's speech should drip with double entendres and hidden meanings, loaded questions and between the lines suggestiveness. This adds entertainment, deepens the meaning of your story, and allows you to express the inexpressible and reach your audience in a way that "straight" dialogue never can.

Whatever your metaphors are, be sure to extend them in as many ways possible. In a poem, often a particular image is used and applied in many different ways in order to extend its meaning to

14

different situations, giving it breadth as well as depth. This is what poets term "extended metaphor."

In a film, it is no different, except the metaphor is played out in different scenes rather than lines and stanzas. For example, if a personal journey is about enduring friendships and a sense of community, then the diner, the actual place where this community is formed, can become the metaphor. To extend the metaphor, you show all kinds of scenes happening there, giving the diner several different aspects of community, such as confiding, dealing with heartbreak, dealing with anti-social behavior, helping each other, making each other laugh, coping with romantic setbacks, etc. And this is what Barry Levinson did in his autobiographical film, DINER.

Integrating the magic of poetic invention into your screenplay as it develops can help with the process immeasurably. As you begin drafting, seeing it in your mind and thinking about its shape and thrust, the process will unfold organically, and ideas will start to flow.

You will find that if you hone in on the main idea and develop a solid metaphor that expresses the core of the movie of your life or the life of your subject, it will naturally inform the plot and characters, serving as a foundation and a focal point.

Once you know your theme and have a metaphor to embody it, you will naturally be able to create the basic story elements of plot and character from which everything else can grow. If you take some time to find your own metaphor, you will be surprised at how much it helps you bring your story to life.

Try This!

Close your eyes, clear your mind, and begin to write quickly, without censoring yourself. Try to write your film story as a poem, and notice whether one consistent metaphor arises. Work on extending the metaphor throughout the poem, seeing how much mileage you can get out of it.

Write this poem "for your eyes only." There's no pressure to produce a great work. You need only express your truth, from the heart, playfully and simply. Treat this as an experiment, a way to discover new possibilities. If you don't come up with much the first time, wait a day or two and try again.

Remember to keep paper by your bedside so that you can begin writing soon after you wake up, and capitalize on the fresh mind, close to your subconscious state and your dreams. Once you're satisfied with the poem, you can look to it for images, scenes, relationships, title ideas and dialogue.

CHAPTER 3:

Translating Real Life into Dramatic Action

How do we begin? Does script development start with character or plot? In fact, there are two theories, or camps, about how one starts a screenplay. One side says that we start with plot, while the other advises that we start with character. If we start with the plot, we see bits and glimpses of the story and we expand on that and then invent a character who will best serve that story.

In the other camp, starting with character, we deeply analyze a character we see in our minds or know in the real world. By asking questions about what that character wants, we can devise a plot that takes this character on his or her necessary journey so that they may attain their goal, or not.

Both of these approaches can work, and both are valid. But what if there were another way, a method which integrates both of the above, but which transcends each and goes to the heart of the story instead? The premise here is that theme can be used as a springboard to create both plot and character. We all have to start somewhere. Why not start with what we have to say? Why not get clear on the message of the story, the reason we are writing it in the first place. What have we learned? This is what, ultimately, if we do our jobs, others will identify with and take away from the experience

17

of watching our film. Knowing our theme first can be a powerful way to focus the story and develop plot and characters that stem from one unified idea.

By theme, I mean the message, or moral, lying deep within your story. This is the nugget of wisdom the audience will walk away with in the end. What does the story teach? Think of traditional sayings, bits of folk wisdom, such as "the grass is always greener," "a bird in hand is worth two in the bush," or "no man is an island."

While these sayings themselves are clichés, the theme they convey are actually universal truths. Find the universal truth lying within your story and you will reach the broadest possible audience.

FOCUS ON YOUR THEME

A woman I know is working on her life story, which includes the suicide of her mother, terrible relationships with stepmothers while she was growing up, and the ultimate salvation she found in her work as a botanist. She describes her theme as "Every day is new," and is realizing that experiencing her mother's suicide when she was nine forced her to find ways to be happy every day, to avoid ever wallowing in depression. Her accomplishments in the field of botany provide the perfect life metaphor for that, since plants don't know how to look back or have regrets, and live essentially and only in the moment. The visual imagery of the plants and forests she has worked in then can become concrete evidence of her philosophy.

What is the moral of the story? Find it first, and then you can build and craft a cohesive script, with a tight plot and engaging characters. The finished product will be more meaningful and

Translating Real Life into Dramatic Action

worthwhile for audiences, leaving them with something thought-provoking to take away.

This is an intuitive, organic approach to the development of plot and character. Ask yourself, what's the point? Write about it every morning for a while, journaling freely, until you find the answer. It may not even be one single answer, but you should after a while find a cohesive core to your story.

Getting clear on your theme can also work as a litmus test. There are many people who have fantastic stories about wild and unbelievably scary, funny, sad, or horrible things that have happened in their lives. As exciting as these stories may be, often things just happen without much growth or learning. But if the question, "What did you take away from it?" is asked, and you can't find a good answer, then it's probably not worth spending six months to a year writing a screenplay on it.

However, if it's a universal theme, something everyone can relate to, then it will have power. You will just know it's something valuable, something that people will respond to. This theme then becomes the seed from which all else, including plot and characters, can grow.

THE "SO WHAT?" TEST

A friend of mine who runs a talent agency in Beverly Hills has a simple benchmark for screenplays, and that is to ask, does it pass the "So what?" test. After he's finished a script or seen a movie, if he has to ask, "So what?" then the script is a pass, or the film is a thumbs down. If he isn't walking away from the experience with a

19

new kernel of truth, ray of hope, or nugget of wisdom, he's not likely to get excited about it for his clients. As we all know, there are far too many films out there that are pointless. They use gratuitous sex and violence to create a huge sensationalist event on the screen but leave us feeling empty inside. Great films make us care, about something or someone, or both.

This doesn't mean that a screenplay should broadcast your message. It's quite the opposite, in fact. The theme, once grasped, has to be tucked away into the back of your mind, only to be dispersed into the story like the seeds of a dandelion in the wind. The irony here is that by letting go, you allow your mind to work subconsciously to create a story that exemplifies, develops, and subtly sings out the core thematic idea.

How do we narrow down the story of our lives, or even one thing that happened in our lives, to find the theme? We can do this either intuitively, based on emotions, or logically, based on our thoughts. Really, this will depend on what kind of thinker you are. Try talking to a close friend about it. Try making lists, journaling. Try taking a long walk or hike and daydreaming on it. If you are so inclined, try asking a higher power for answers and insight.

In the best possible scenario, you will combine logic and emotion to find the theme of your story. Take some time and ask yourself on an emotional level, what matters most? What do you have to say to the world, based on your life experience? What is in your heart? Then, using your critical mind, ask yourself whether you have something fresh to say, and a fresh way of saying it. Ask yourself what would be the most entertaining way to get your heart's song across to the world.

The next step is to create a paragraph for yourself on the subject of your script's theme. Start with "This script is about…" and write on that. Here is where you get to be philosophical. You don't need to talk about the action or the plot, just the ideas, lessons and abstract outcomes you want your story to convey. Be pedantic, be obvious, state it overtly to yourself, so that you are clear on the meaning and the message. Then, put this paragraph away. Close enough for you to glance at it from time to time, but far enough away so that it does not directly touch your screenplay pages.

Once you have a paragraph or so of tightly written message material, you can more easily imagine a character and storyline that will exemplify that theme. For instance, if the message is, "The truth is not always meant to be told," then you have character and plot springing from that organically. It's easy to see that at least one character in your story needs to be someone who always tells the truth no matter what, and another character will withhold the truth for good reason. And it's equally easy to see that the story must embroil these two characters in a situation where the truth teller suffers consequences of his actions and the withholder of truth is redeemed.

The benefits of this approach are that you end up with a more unified film, where content dictates form and you are more likely to craft a work of art with your story rather than a formulaic rehash of other films, or a heavy-handed, obvious version of your life story. Besides, now your script will have a point, and this message will help you focus your storyline and develop your characters with interesting dimension. People will come out of the theaters enjoying not just the entertainment of the ride, but also the message that the film conveys.

FIND THE BEST DESIGN

As any good architect will tell you that form should follow function, especially if you're trying to build something solid. This is really just another way of saying that story (plot and character) should follow theme. Take a look at the film INVICTUS as an example of how plot and character can spring from theme. When you have subject matter that contains hordes of philosophical, political and psychological complexities, such as the story of Nelson Mandela's efforts to unite South Africans in common support for their national rugby team, the most elegant way to lay out your story is to follow several different characters, show the events from many perspectives, and let the truth then speak for itself.

The Clint Eastwood-helmed film, which stars Morgan Freeman as Mandela and Matt Damon as Francois Pienaar, captain of the Springboks, is propelled by the theme of unifying a segregated country. Mandela is trying to bring together the blacks and whites, and the story unfolds from a myriad of perspectives: Mandela's, Pienaar's, the team of Mandela's bodyguards, and in smaller proportions, Mandela's assistant, some taxi drivers dealing with a street kid, and Mandela's wife, whom he is separated from. Within each of these various POV's, you'll find a racial mix; some of the bodyguards are white and some are black, and Pienaar's housekeeper is black.

As the story progresses, the black and white factions are brought closer together through the shared experience of sports enthusiasm. They all eventually manage to put their differences aside and root for the South African team to win the World Cup. The film's design lends itself well for study of a true story's adaptation into screenplay. The multi-faceted structure really works, and the film delivers a potent emotional punch.

The theme of this film might be stated as, "We need to set aside our differences and come together for a common cause." Structurally, form follows function as the various characters literally and figuratively "come together" through the conflict that arises on Mandela's journey towards unification of the country. By focusing on the World Cup, the story conveys our commonalities and our humanity. Without telling, the action reveals the theme. The message is demonstrated, not preached.

Every story has its own best design. The key to finding it lies in discovering the theme. What are you trying to say? Whatever that is, naming it will allow you to start playing with story, plot, and character development in a way that is organic, yet keeps your script focused and propelled by the truth.

To create an organic drama, one that has cohesion and power, unity and flow, the plot should stem from the motivations that drive the characters, and the situations which exemplify the themes. What the characters want can be translated into action by designing scenes that show them pursuing their goals. These goals can and should be quirky, offbeat, and unique. But above all, they need to be concrete, physical, and externalized into dramatic action.

FIND THE OPPOSING FORCES

Conflict, which can be defined as the intersection between protagonist and antagonistic forces, can be either internal or external. External conflict is defined as conflict with another person, an institution, or nature. Since everything in a film must be seen and heard rather than thought about, most everything has to be externalized in your screenplay. Thus, there are usually good guys and bad guys in action films and Westerns, someone or something coming between two lovers in romantic comedies, and some kind of manifestation of evil in most dramas.

Internal conflict is any issue that a person might be wrestling with within themselves, such as whether to quit a job, leave a spouse, forgive someone, or become more spontaneous. While outer conflict can translate to the screen literally, inner conflict must be personified and externalized into dramatic action. This is where your imagination must come into play.

If you are trying to dramatize an internal conflict, such as the need for self-acceptance or a desire to attain autonomy, resolution or acceptance, you need to dream up scenes that exemplify and manifest your internal experience and journey. Relationships, situations, adventures and conversations all provide opportunities to dramatize, and to show rather than tell about a character evolving or embarking upon a personal journey.

You start with a personal experience you want to convey in a film. Perhaps you had a troubled relationship with a parent. Perhaps

24

you endured hardship for a period of time, through poverty, abuse, or political oppression. Most people are "survivors" of one sort or another. What have you survived? Chances are, others have endured similar challenges and are interested in how you overcame all those obstacles.

Or perhaps there is just a question nagging at you about how things worked out, an unresolved issue regarding a relationship with a lover, choices made in your career, or some other inner conflict that is as of yet unresolved. The key is to isolate that inner conflict and let it be the inspiration point for imagining a connected and developing series of scenes (the plot) and a hook to hang the action on, (the frame) which will evoke the emotional content and convey the emotional journey of the true story.

Coming up with conflict in a true story is essential, and often difficult, because in real life, the face-off between antagonist and protagonist forces is not always clear. In AMELIA, the writers present many obstacles to her goals of flying – the need to raise money and the compromises she must make, a man who loves her and wants her to stay alive, and a world of commercialism, which tries to prevent her from pursuing her dreams at every turn. But she overcomes these obstacles with her attitude of freedom – she doesn't care what others think, she refuses to bow to convention, and in these ways she emulates again and again the theme of freedom at all costs.

BEGINNING, MIDDLE AND END

The beginning, middle and end of a good story don't always

correspond with the chronology of events as they happened in real life. In fact, it's better if they don't. Because a good story needs to be manipulated, so it can take on a new shape.

How do you find a structure for your story? How do you come up with a strong narrative arc? How do you get a firm handle on the beginning, middle and end? One way to see your way through is to allow your theme to guide you. What are you hoping to say? What is your story about? What is the purpose, or point? Once you have clarified that in your mind, you can stand back and let your theme inform your structure. Here is where it becomes intuitive rather than rational.

For instance, if I was trying to show the importance of coming to terms with the past and letting go of shame in order to live fully in the present, I might structure my story so that it represents that idea. I could, for instance, have the whole story take place in one day, beginning at dawn when the heroine wakes up, and ending it at midnight when she goes back to sleep. The story could take place over one single day, but within that day flashbacks would allow her to face and come to terms with parts of her past that she is ashamed of. That's the story in one of my screenplays THE DAY SHE DROVE ME. It's her 30th birthday, and her boyfriend has just proposed to her, but she's afraid to accept because her past still haunts her. In the course of one day, all that she's been hiding from her boyfriend comes to light, and in the end she finds acceptance. Before it can all be happily resolved, however, first there has to be a conflict-ridden middle, where all of the heroine's inner demons are manifested in the mess and chaos of a relationship gone awry.

In this way, the idea of accepting the past in order to move forward is shaped into story, with a sequence of events that in no way corresponds with the chronology of real events in my life, but instead evokes the idea of the story and works more like a song than a speech, capturing the essence of my truth without recounting things exactly as they happened.

Think about how, in your true story, you may be getting stuck on telling it just as it happened. Perhaps you need to step back, free yourself from chronology, and try approaching structure from a more abstract, idea-centered place. Ask yourself first what the story is about, what lessons can be learned from it, and see if you can't come up with a plotline that poetically conveys your theme.

To put yourself in the right frame of mind, pretend you are one of the millions of moviegoers who is spending their hard earned cash on a two hour experience. You want to be wowed. You want to be mesmerized, and in some small way, you want to be changed and transformed by the events you see unfolding on the screen.

Try This!

Answer these questions about your screenplay:

Who wants what?

Who or what is in their way?

How do they overcome these obstacles to achieve their goals?

Write down as many possibilities as you can think of to "storify" your personal themes. Write fast and freely, with no concern for grammar or punctuation. No one will read this but you. Nothing has to make sense and none of the ideas have to be good (although some of them will be, if only by accident) Trust the writing process, and write for fifteen minutes on each question.

CHAPTER 4:

Developing Engaging Characters from Real People

In a movie based on real life, the characters are based on real people, usually people we know well, and this is a great way to begin. It offers a model with which to mold a new, larger than life dramatic character, within the confines of story. But in order to make the leap from real people to great roles, the characters need to be shaped so that they serve the story. This means that their motivations need to drive the story, their quirks and neuroses must inform the twists and turns, and their hidden desires, whims and unique traits should lend subtext to the scenes. In this way, the characters start out real, but then become imagined in a totally new way. The roles remain real in essence and ultimately feel believable, while also emerging as larger than life on the page.

Tom Schulman, screenwriter of DEAD POETS SOCIETY, once wrote, "Everything I write is autobiographical in the sense that I shape characters only from the people I know in my life. They start out as people I know and then they change, as the story changes them." The idea is to make the leap from real person to developed character. A character can capture the essence of the real person, but it's never going to feel exactly the same. A character will have a few memorable traits and will change in one focused way along the

29

storyline, whereas a person is a complex, ever-changing organism. There is a depth and a breadth to a living being that a character can only briefly suggest.

What this means for the autobiographical and biographical screenwriter is that there needs to be a sharp focus on certain aspects of the character, and these need to be magnified, stressed, and exemplified in their behavior. Their inner traits, the essence of their personality, need to be identified by you, the writer, but then they need to be made manifest in your character's actions. Because in film, actions are all we have. We might have a character who represents a certain theme in our minds, but that message has to be translated into actions, so that every scene is filled with them demonstrating the idea in their behavior, dialogue, choices and gestures.

In the film SECRETARIAT, for example, Penny Chenery, played by Diane Lane, is making manifest the inner theme of "the importance of going for it," as exemplified both by her horse's determination and her own. At one point, she even says, "it's about life being ahead of you, and you run at it." When she faces the external obstacle of a lost race, she refuses to give up. We see her walk to the stable where the colt was born, and hear in her mind the voices of the trainer and keeper who were stunned at the colt's pizzazz during his very first moments of life. We see her staring at the horse himself, and then going out to help groom him. She picks up the towel, literally and figuratively, and helps spread the soap and water.

It is in this action that we know she will never "throw in the towel," i.e., give up. We see it and feel it, because the character is showing commitment in that moment. Had she just talked about it, we would understand her determination cerebrally, but we wouldn't feel it in our gut, and it wouldn't have been a memorable film moment, or ultimately helped make the role an appealing one for the actress.

It's a little known fact by the general public that almost all films get made for one reason and one reason only: because an actor wants the role. The producers and financiers who have decided to bankroll a movie will first approach actors to try and garner their interest. They will try and get a Matt Damon or a Hillary Swank on board first, and then put the rest of the package together.

So, first a producer will take a terrific screenplay to the talent agencies. The agents read it and send that script to their clients, the actors. Once a client has signed on, everything else can move forward. The trades (*Variety* and *The Hollywood Reporter*) soon announce that the film is readying for production, and reveal who is attached, usually with a "pay or play" deal. This term means that the actor is guaranteed a certain salary, regardless of whether the film is actually made or not, and whether the actor is replaced by the studios or not. Since an actor sacrifices other roles and opportunities by committing to a long time period to make a film, they need this guarantee. Once the producers make a pay or play offer to someone, and it's accepted, this means that a serious deal has been made and the film has a good chance of moving forward. What all this means is that your script must first and foremost appeal to an actor.

One of the nuances of the casting process is that producers make offers to actors based on their bankability, i.e. how much their past few movies have made at the box office. How much an actor's movie made last time will dictate what the producers think the next movie starring the same actor will make. Hence the phrase, "What has he done lately?"

By the same turn, in order to secure and advance their career, actors are drawn to roles that will make the most money at the box office. They look for a certain level of commercial appeal to keep their name safe, because they know that it's not only their performance that will keep crowds coming. It's also the quality of the script, and the attractiveness of the story. They want the best script possible, with the highest entertainment value, and they also want the best role possible, one that will showcase their talents. They must factor all of these things in to protect and preserve their career.

There are many other factors that influence an actor's decision to sign on. Among them are wanting to work with someone they've never worked with, wanting to work with someone they have worked with and love, wanting to do comedy if they fear being pigeonholed as a dramatic actor, or vice versa, wanting to work in a particular country if the film is set there, wanting to portray a role that speaks to a certain theme if it's an issue going on in their lives, wanting to prove their chops, needing to make money to pay the bills, and wanting to work with a certain director because they admire them.

Here is an excerpt from a recent article in *The Hollywood Reporter*, which illustrates the all importance element of casting:

"CANNES -- Al Pacino is joining the cast of Fiore Films' Gotti: Three Generations, the true-life crime saga, which is set to star John Travolta as John Gotti Sr. Pacino, who knows his way away mob families having starring in The Godfather trilogy, will play Gambino crime family underboss Neil Dellacroce, an associate and mentor to Gotti Sr. The project reteams Pacino with Barry Levinson, who has stepped in to direct, and who recently guided Pacino through the Emmy-winning HBO telefilm You Don't Know Jack.

Other key roles that have been cast include that of Gotti Sr.'s wife Victoria, who will be played by Travolta's real-life wife Kelly Preston; Angel Gotti, the daughter of John Sr. and Victoria, who will be played by the Travoltas' daughter Ella Bleu Travolta; Gotti Sr.'s associate Angelo Ruggiero, who will be played by Joe Pesci; and Kim Gotti, John Gotti Jr.'s wife, who will be played by Lindsay Lohan." (*Hollywood Reporter* 5/13/2011 by Gregg Kilday)

For the studios and financiers, it is about the bottom line. For the actor, it is about their career. But for the writer, it is about fleshing out the characters so that they come alive on the page and can ultimately be manifested into exciting and unforgettable roles for actors. So much depends on the actor connecting with the character in the script that you need to take this aspect very seriously if you want to see your story reach the big screen.

Just as a story needs to be a metaphor for life, characters need to be metaphors for real people, embodying both the universal and the unique traits of a real person. Great screen characters need to feel authentic, and yet be larger than life at the same time. An actor wants to play a role that is memorable in the minds of filmgoers. That means the characters' emotional journeys need to be taken to the extreme, yet in a way that is believable. What we're looking for here is depth and breadth.

One of the most fundamental aspects of being human is to want things. And because drama is made from the conflict which arises when characters pursue their goals, the clarification of a character's desires is crucial. You will need to spend some time developing your character's motivations, and then making it clear to the audience what that character needs and wants. This is done through action, since motivations are revealed when the character does or says something in order to pursue his or her goal. Character is revealed through conflict; it is in the character's response to conflict that we learn what makes them tick.

Actors want vehicles to showcase their talent. They want levels to play, conflict, complexity, subtext, and the desire to attain things that which are at odds with each other, forcing them to make moral choices. They want unique roles which have never been seen before, and they want to be put in impossible situations, reacting with a wide range of feelings.

Another paradox of characterization is that a great character has never been seen before, and yet feels familiar. When we meet someone new, we notice their surprising quirks, unusual gestures, some odd way of saying something, and if we really tune in, we can sense that their brain thinks differently than ours, in a way that is totally unique to that individual. At the same time, we will usually recognize something in them that is like us, something we can relate to. Not always, but often, this is true. What we recognize is their humanity. Well developed characters will surprise us with their humanity, not just when we read the story, but even as we write it.

WHAT TOUCHES YOU?

In the film HACHIKO: A DOG'S TALE we are compelled to watch a film about a dog. That's right, a dog, and this is not an animated or children's film. Why do we watch Hachi's story? Because of the single-minded devotion of this dog, who bonds so fiercely to his owner, a professor who lives in the country but works in the city. The professor rescues him as a puppy from the train station, raises him, and then is happily surprised when his dog runs several blocks from their house to the train station every day at 5:00 p.m. to greet him when he arrives home from work.

But the real story begins after the professor dies, when this dog returns every day to the train station at the same time to wait for him. For nine years. Until his death, right there on the ledge at the train station. That's the whole story. It's not much of a story, actually. But what makes Hachi a great character? I think it is simply that his story touches us, awakens our sense of purpose, and reminds us to rise above our circumstances and find a higher calling.

The story of Hachiko is based on a real life professor in Japan, but the film is set in upstate New York and stars Richard Gere and Joan Allen, and was directed by Lasse Halstrom. The structure of the screenplay is a bit cumbersome, mainly because you are waiting for the professor to die for the first half of the film, with no clue as to how he will die and no tension surrounding his death or his relationship with the dog. There is some tension brought on by the professor's wife (Allen) who doesn't really want the dog, but for the most part, the family is portrayed as happy, calm, and successful. Not much drama there.

Low conflict and tension aside, the film does a great job of depicting Hachi's character and paints a clear picture of Hachi's experience, so that when we see the dog's devotional sprint to the train station every day after his master dies, we believe it, and we fall in love. We relate to and identify with the universal emotion of loyalty.

When you watch AMELIA, notice how alcoholism plays into and informs Amelia's character at every turn, and helps the role become much more nuanced. She is trying to maintain control at all times. She tells Noonan, her navigator, that the only man she ever truly loved unconditionally was her father, and he was a drunk who let her down throughout her life. She lets it be known that she has zero tolerance for it now. This theme both informs her character and gives a certain direction to the plot, because it affects the choices she makes, which in turn affect the story.

In HACHIKO, the theme can be stated as "loyalty and devotion will triumph even in death." In AMELIA, it might be seen as "freedom is worth pursuing at all costs." In both of these films, as well as many other well-written films based on true stories, theme serves as a springboard for both character and plot. It's a lesson worth lingering on when we're shaping true story into screenplay.

For the next few days, notice when you are moved, and by what. What do these things have in common? Where is your soft spot? We all have unique interests and passions, but on the other hand, the things that move us as human beings are surprisingly similar. Most of us are touched by true love, dedication, courage, and transcendent moments.

To write a great character, find what touches you about them. Keep in mind that what touches you is ultimately what will touch others, because the more you mine for the gold in your own heart, the more likely it is that your characters will convey those emotions to your audience in universal ways.

Characters need to be focused and consistent. But we also need to allow them to be many things at once, and not pigeonhole them into a one-dimensional portrait. We need to give them opportunities to show their different moods and reactions, their strengths and weaknesses, their quirks - all the things that make them odd, unique, weird even, and interesting. We've established that actors make the world go 'round in Hollywood. So give your actors something they can really chew on. Keep adding dimensions and layers, and keep going for the most unique strokes you can think of as you paint their portraits in your screenplay.

Dig deep in your heart for original, authentic ways your characters can express themselves. Take who they really are or were and morph them into something grander and more involving. Try to surprise us, or even better, shock us into understanding your character so that he or she will live on in our minds and join the long list of roles which have played out in film history and become truly memorable.

Try This!

Write a detailed biography about your main character, getting down everything you can think of regarding their background and personality. Include not only their physical and sociological descriptions, but also their psychology. Think about their economics, their tastes, passions, vices, and obsessions.

What makes them tick? What are their secret hopes and dreams? What is their secret vice? Most importantly, what makes them unique?

Write answers to these questions as you develop and write the script. Do it for each of your characters. This will help make the characters come alive, so that they live and breathe.

CHAPTER 5:

Shaping the Plot Along a Story Spine

Movies have their own unique structure, a structure that in no way resembles a real life. If we're writing about ourselves or another person, we need to study the basic shape of a movie and then work to capture a particular journey, which can become the essence of the screen story and the spine of the plot. We need to find the beginning, middle and end, and we need to present the action so that it has a dramatic build. The stakes will be high for the hero or heroine from the outset. The hurdles will get higher and higher as the story unfolds. And through it all, the main character will grow and change. These are just a few of the essential elements in a screen story that you will need to pay attention to every step of the way.

To make the transition from real life to a plotline, the first step is to clarify what one small aspect of the true story calls out to be dramatized. An entire life is far too large in scope for a film; even a decade or a year contains too much activity, detail and plot. A movie is approximately two hours, and can only capture a glimpse of the truth as it happened. All a film can ever do is encapsulate one significant event or situation, or a series of related events which have meaning or value on their own.

We find this one event or situation of significance through

the exploration of our theme. When we focus in on what it is we want our story to convey, we should begin to see that there is only so much of our whole life story that needs to be told to convey that theme.

FIND THE SPINE

If you want to write a tight, compelling screenplay, it has to be focused along a story spine. What is the story spine? It is both character and plot, and it is the essence of the story. Picture the protagonist's main journey. Now picture a human being's spine. It is straight, firm, and strong, yet it is also the base from which everything else moves.

The trouble with real life is that most people live to be over 80 years old. A film is only two hours long. If you try to squeeze too many themes or situations into a 120 page screenplay document, you end up with an episodic whirlwind of a story. It will have no overall through-line, no uniting theme, and the narrative arc will be weak. What's needed is a unifying idea, a core to the plot, which ties it all together and gives the story cohesion. Different things can happen, of course, but they all must somehow relate to one overriding action. This main action is closely aligned with the goal of the protagonist, and it should reflect a thematic question that is being explored.

The abstract concept of story is made concrete in the hero's journey, which is also the main plot, or, as Aristotle called it, the one unified action. In his seminal work, *The Poetics*, Aristotle writes, "The plot…must imitate one action…the structural union of the parts being such that, if any one of them is displaced or removed, the whole will be disjointed and disturbed."

When he writes about this unified action, Aristotle isn't referring to car crashes, fights or helicopter stunts. The action refers to the motivation of the protagonist, and all of the things he or she does to achieve or not achieve the objective. "Who wants what?" and "how do they try to get it?" must be asked, again and again. It's about character and motivation.

In the Greek tragedy *Oedipus Rex,* Oedipus' one main action is to find the slayer of the King of Thebes in order to assuage the gods and end the plague.

In DINER, the one main action is for a group of men to grow up, and in particular, for one of them to take the plunge and get married. While this film eschews a traditional narrative, every scene in some way has to do with this one main action and the story coheres to that spine, albeit episodically and without traditional structure.

How do we shape the plot along a story spine? We generate as many ideas as possible to tell the story and then we examine each scene idea, making sure that it indeed furthers this one main action. Everything must fit, must relate and must somehow echo and resonate with the main idea. Then, in order to organize the scenes, create flow and build story momentum, we begin to arrange our story according to the dramatic shape of a three-act structure.

THREE-ACT STRUCTURE

Traditional dramatic narrative takes a form, a shape, which helps the audience follow a story according to their expectations, and ultimately makes the story more engaging and accessible. This shape is both simple and complex: it entails having a beginning, middle and end, but within that simple framework, there is much complexity. Each act must rise and fall and each scene within that act must also have a set up, development, climax and resolution.

We start with events, scenes and situations. Then we just have to shape those events into a plot with a three act structure – a beginning, middle, and end. It can be quite a puzzle do decide how to arrange all of our scenes and situations into a dramatic narrative. But one way to approach the puzzle is to look at models. If we take a look at some of the approaches that the masters of dramatic structure have taken, we can pick and choose what works for us, and most importantly, we can begin to imagine how the events of our own lives will fit into a three-act structure that is uniquely ours, tailored specifically to our themes and storyline.

When you're trying to structure your plot, you should immerse yourself in different models for structure. Study the diagrams, think about the shapes that different stories make. Some books that are very useful and inspirational to study include: Aristotle's *The Poetics*, Sophocles' *Oedipus Rex*, Joseph Campbell's *The Hero with a Thousand Faces*, Robert McKee's *Story*, Linda Seger's *The Art of Adaptation: Turning Fact and Fiction into Film*, Tristine Rainer's *Your Life as Story*, and Syd Field's *Screenplay*.

Start with Joseph Campbell's archetypal approach to structure. In his *Hero With a Thousand Faces*, he presents a structure for the hero's journey. It is broken down into three parts, or acts:

Departure

Initiation

Return

Within each act, there are movements which can be specifically identified.

<u>Act I</u>

> The Call to Adventure
>
> Refusal of the Call
>
> Supernatural Aid
>
> The Crossing of the First Threshold
>
> The Belly of the Whale

<u>Act II</u>

> The Road of Trials
>
> The Meeting with the Goddess
>
> Woman as the Temptress
>
> Atonement with the Father
>
> Apotheosis
>
> The Ultimate Boon

<u>Act III</u>

> Refusal of the Return
>
> The Magic Flight
>
> Rescue from Without
>
> The Crossing of the Return Threshold
>
> Master of the Two Worlds
>
> Freedom to Live

(Campbell, Joseph. The Hero With a Thousand Faces. Princeton: Bollingen, 1972.)

You may be looking at the above outline and wondering how in the world you can relate these elements to your own true story. But if you immerse yourself in Campbell's work and feel your way through his description of the mythic journey, it will help you identify your own version of this story structure. Your story probably won't have an actual goddess, temptress, or magic flight. But in your own journey or that of the real person you are writing about, there are probably similarities to these archetypal characters and plot points.

Author and writing teacher Shari Caudron offers another way to craft your plot in her workshop "The Story Only You Can Tell." She draws upon Campbell's work and updates it for a new era, suggesting that we answer the following questions through a series of 10-15 minute free-writes:

*Who is the main character?

* What was their "normal" life like before the inciting incident?

* What is the situation they find themselves in?

* What do they want?

* Who are the other key characters? (Identify allies, mentors and adversaries)

* What are the obstacles the main character faces?

* What is the final turning point/climax?

* How is the main character changed?

To find your story's spine, try to focus on each of these questions for 10-15 minutes at a time, free-writing all of your thoughts and responses as they come to mind.

Whatever you're writing, at a certain point you need to work on structure, ask yourself where it's weak, and fortify the narrative storyline so that it rises and falls, builds and engages, and ultimately satisfies the audience.

THE DRAMATIC QUESTION

After deciding which aspect of personal experience you want to focus on and how you will shape it along a story spine, you will need to transform it into a dramatic question. In a film, the audience is hooked in early on by the element of suspense, whether the genre is comedy, drama, or thriller. This element of suspense is necessary to keep people engaged in the film, and it is rooted in the presentation of a dramatic question, such as, "Will he get the girl?" "Will she survive out in the wilderness?" or "Will the family ever be reunited?" This question is never asked outright; instead it is buried in the subtext of dramatic scenes.

Clarifying the dramatic question helps you see not only what the core story dilemma is, but also what the possibilities might be for storylines. A dramatic question tells us who wants what and suggests the obstacles that a character must overcome to get it. This, in turn, is what creates that one indispensable element of drama: conflict.

THE PLEASURES OF THE GENRE

A screenwriting instructor of mine used to talk quite a bit about what he called "delivering the pleasures of the genre." He meant that, as a screenwriter, you need to be clear on your genre and then be honest with yourself about whether the script fulfills all of the expectations your audience will have when they go to see your movie. Those expectations come about as a result of the genre you've chosen to write in, which you set up at the very beginning of your film and carry all the way through. Each genre comes with its own set of expectations. For instance, in a:

- o Love Story - The romantic pair meet, then in some way separate or break apart, and then in the end, must reunite in order to fulfill the genre's expectations.

- o Mystery - Someone is killed early in the story and then someone else pursues the identity of the killer.

- o Thriller - A tone of suspense is established from the start and sustained throughout the story, in which someone or more than one person is in a life-threatening situation.

- o Action/Adventure - Lots of action, of course, and the more violent the better. Shane Black (screenwriter, LETHAL WEAPON, LAST BOY SCOUT, and many others) is quoted as saying that the key to writing good action is reversals (and he should know).

- o Fish out of Water - This genre offers a multitude of possibilities and can be taken in many directions, but the key expectation is that someone or something will be placed in an environment that is totally unfamiliar and will need to adapt in some way.

Probably, your true story offers some kind of combination or hybrid of these genres. There might be drama and romance and action and suspense. In this case, you can draw upon many different types of films for inspiration and guidance. Define your hybrid genre, such as action-romantic-comedy, and then ask yourself, "What are the pleasures of this genre?" And then ask, "How can I deliver them to my audience?" You'll find that the answers will help lead you to the development of a strong story spine.

Try This!

On a legal size piece of paper held lengthwise, draw a line across the middle that curves up and down, like an arc. It should look something like the shape of a dinosaur's back. Divide the line into four equally spaced sections. Now, use this as the backbone of your story, writing down the main events that happen in Act I, early Act II, late Act II, and Act III. These will correlate to pages 1-30, 31-60, 61-90, and 91-120 of your screenplay.

Fill in the spaces above and below the arc, jotting down scenes and situations for your main characters and your main plot. For each section, make a list of as many events and possible scenes as you can. Don't worry about how they will merge or be strung together just yet. Let them sit next to each other on the page, and float in space a bit, before you begin to refine this storyline even further.

CHAPTER 6:

Choosing What to Leave out in the Interest of Story

When we're trying to get down a filmic version of reality, we are often flooded with details which seem important and necessary to the telling of the story. What someone wore, exactly what they said, what sort of car they drove or what music was playing are all examples of details that seem important, but which actually can cloud the writer's task of designing the story. We want to be sure to focus on the forest first, and the trees later.

All of these details will help immensely with description, supporting roles, settings, and small bits of texture within the scenes. But this minutia cannot be the focus when you're trying to plan, outline and identify the main storyline for the movie. Let them come to mind, as they naturally will, while you write. But in the early, developmental stages of writing, they should be set aside. Don't get too bogged down in the details until the first draft is complete. Keep jotting everything down on 3x5 cards, or a notes file on the computer, and save them for later.

A lot of things have happened to you in your life since you were born. But the road to building an engaging screenplay means narrowing down the scope of the story you are trying to tell. After you've given your story shape along a spine, the next step is deciding what to leave out. This means tightening your focus, from the countless things that have happened to you, to only those things which are most evocative of the theme you are going to convey in this film.

In the book which was the basis for the film RUNNING WITH SCISSORS, for example, there are explicit sexual acts, such as homosexual rape and lesbian oral sex, which are toned down quite a bit for the film. This is because in a film, less is more. A little goes a long way, and often the more subtle choice is best. Ratings are also a factor of course, and for the broadest possible audience, you'll need to limit gratuitous sex, language and violence.

Another thing to consider when you are deciding what to put in and what to leave out is the story's tone. The script will have a certain feeling to it, a mood, and although the scenes will rise and fall, be funny or sad, exciting or somber, the overall tone of the piece needs to have a sense of unity. In order to have a successful tone, writers need to choose only scenes that will fit in with the main thrust of the story, and which synthesize well with the feeling of the rest of the piece.

You have your story's spine charted out, and your theme, or story message in mind. Use these to guide you towards choices that will keep your story coherent and unified. Remember, too, that often we don't know what the story is all about, what belongs and what doesn't, until we've written a draft, and begun to revise it. It is in the revisions, and later the editing, that we become more solid about what this story is and what it isn't. The story begins to know itself and it will tell us what fits and what needs to be let go. We just need to listen.

Along the way, however, as you are planning and drafting, you can cultivate selectivity by asking yourself which scenes further the plot. Try to only include those scenes that in some way move the story forward. As an exercise, list every scene you plan to include in the film. Then ask yourself for every scene, how does this advance the plot? Reveal character? And provide entertainment? If it doesn't do all three of these things, then you either need to find a way to make the scene stronger, or cut it.

In a whole life, many people come and go. So many people matter and have influenced you, or your main character. But in a film story, characters must be chosen with excruciating care. Often, one or more characters need to be cut out of the story in the interest of keeping the narrative focused. It's not unusual for two or more characters to be combined into a composite. This is a good option when several characters have similarities and tend to represent shared traits in your mind.

Situations are different from scenes in that they are less specific and more abstract. But they are another element to consider when it comes to paring down the story, and making tough choices about what to put in and what to leave out.

For example, perhaps I'm writing a film about my journey towards self-acceptance, and one of the situations I want to depict in the story is the fact that I could never stand up to my brother. A scene of him cutting half my hair off when I was seven, and me cowering quietly, would be a good one to include. I may have a couple of other scenes that elucidate this situation in some way, and I would arrange these so that they build to a boiling point.

However, in this same story, the situation of my brother's summer job as a pet sitter would not fit in, as it does not directly relate to or in any way feed the main story of my journey towards self-acceptance. It may be funny, or sad, and develop his character. But this is not a story about his character. It's a story about my journey towards self-acceptance, right? Therefore, unless it somehow helps develop the idea of my self-acceptance, it's probably irrelevant to the main action.

THE LENS OF LOVE

In composition classes and story development, there is something known as the "controlling idea." Whether it is overtly stated or subtly implied, a good essay or film will always convey meaning through it. When we are writing from our own true stories, it is important to hone and sharpen our controlling idea and to shape our entire storyline in correlation with it. This also helps us leave scenes by the wayside which don't cohere to the rest of the piece.

THE LAST STATION, a film by Michael Hoffman, is based on a biographical novel by Jay Parini about Leo Tolstoy. The film offers some important lessons for autobiographical and biographical screenwriters as it tells the story of how Tolstoy plans to settle his estate after his death. Had the filmmakers just given us the facts, and shown us the events which occurred, this would have been a very long, boring film. But instead, they romanticized and dramatized it, telling it through the lens of love, and the stars, Mirren and Plummer, ended up nominated for numerous high profile awards.

The controlling idea that love is the most important philosophy of all is blatantly stated in the film's opening. Over black, we see the words "All, everything that I understand, I understand only because I love." This is a quote from Leo Tolstoy himself, which guides and propels the rest of this historical biopic about the author.

When you watch the film, notice how this theme is developed throughout the story. Everything that happens is in direct relationship to this idea. Notice also how the story is seen through the eyes of McAvoy's Valentin, a celibate young man who takes a job as Tolstoy's new secretary. He soon strikes up a passionate affair with a rebellious member of the agrarian Tolstoy commune. This choice of narrator and subplot serve to deepen and develop the controlling idea even further.

The structuring of this lovely film helps us get a grasp on the line between fact and fiction. When structuring true story into screenplay, what matters is the theme that will propel and give shape to the events portrayed.

What is your controlling idea? How will you distort, shape and focus the massive amount of material that is your life, or the real life of someone else whom you have chosen to write about?

Try This!

A log line is one long sentence that contains the overview of your story's beginning, middle and end. It's that blurb you find on the screen or web page when you're deciding whether or not to watch a movie.

Now that you have your story spine charted out, you are ready to write your log line. Jot down the main action of your story in one sentence. Write this in present tense, such as, "When her boyfriend proposes to her on her 30th birthday, a woman decides to take him on a drive to all the places she's ever lived, and ultimately she has to face her past in order to move forward."

You may have to work on it for a while. After you get a draft, let it sit for a day or two and then rewrite it. Make sure it captures the ideas of who wants what, who or what is getting in their way, and how they overcome obstacles. Now, tape your log line up somewhere close to your computer. As you compile and organize your story, you can repeatedly refer to it. Let it help you stay on track.

Chapter 7:

Charting the Subplots to Create Cohesive Layers

One of your goals as a true story screenwriter should be to take all of the many layers of personal experience in your story and meld them together into one cohesive plot line. This one main line contains many layers, or subplots, but all of these subplots need to blend smoothly with your story's main spine.

A well-built screenplay puts forth a main plot and supports it with at least one, and usually several subplots. While the main plot grabs us with a strong dramatic question and keeps us thoroughly engaged with the main characters, subplots add nuance as they harmonize with the main plot.

For the autobiographical and biographical screenwriter, these layers help to expand the story so that more details from one's life can be used. At the same time, they help contain those details along focused plot lines so that the story does not feel "all over the place."

Subplots make the story more layered and add depth by addressing different dimensions of the character and his or her story. While a main plot might be about getting revenge against someone, a subplot could show the journey of healing and forgiveness for the wrongdoing. In order to make all the subplots resonate with each other, it's important to build storylines that in some way bounce off each other, as variations on a common theme.

Remember, too, that in many great stories, there's not just one theme, but several, closely connected themes. This will keep your screenplay from getting pedantic or preachy. Sometimes different themes conflict with each other, or contrast in some way. This can reveal the gray area and make the story much more interesting and realistic. The important thing is that there is some complexity, and that questions are raised as the growth of the character is shown.

To design your whole story, try charting all the possible subplots in order to develop smooth, cohesive layers. Think about these as radiating out like concentric circles, from the most personal inner journey of growth by the main character (externalized and dramatized into the actions he or she takes) to relationship conflicts with others, to a societal relationship as exemplified by the authorities, government or other institutions of the world around them.

Another method is to draw three or four lines across a page, identify each line as a plotline, and then chart across each line the major plot turns. This visual aid can help you see how the different plots will intersect. You might want to pick up a pack of 11x14 blank paper for this exercise. Holding it lengthwise, try to map your storylines out on the page. This graphic representation can clarify a process that might otherwise grow muddled, and literally help you shape your story.

It also helps to think about tone and pacing. For instance, if the main storyline contains a long, heavy-hearted scene, you might want to follow it with a shorter, more upbeat scene, to give the audience a chance to take a breath, and keep the story from dragging or feeling too "down" for too long.

All of your story's layers should be developed to tell the truth of your experience while simultaneously following the dramatic structure of set up, development and resolution. As the story progresses, the sense of conflict and tension builds and the stakes continue to be raised along each plot line, until the climax. Then, if possible, all of the individual storylines reach their breaking point and erupt with a kind of synchronicity. The result is a new outlook, a ray of hope, and an answer to the initial dramatic question which was raised in the beginning of the story.

For instance, in RUNNING WITH SCISSORS, the story follows Augusten's main relationship with his parents, his romantic relationship with a man, and his friendship with a girl his own age. Each of these plotlines builds dramatically as the story progresses. And each adds dimension to the main story of Augusten coming of age, while cohering together and providing counterpoint to each other.

Think of a subplot as a minor situation. It needs to be something that will rub up against the main story, and help move it forward. While this situation probably would not form a movie by itself, it can flesh out the main story arc, and help define your main character's emotional journey. In order to dramatize it, you'll have to dream up, from both memory and imagination, scenes that personify the emotional truth of what really happened. Your goal is to find a way for this smaller story to provide counterpoint and variety to the larger story, but still keeping it coherent, so it all holds together.

The subplot is often an opportunity to show the heart and soul of your story. For example, in my script, THE DAY SHE DROVE ME, the main storyline is about a young woman struggling with her past in order to decide whether to accept a marriage proposal. The subplot is the story of her boyfriend's parents, who are coming to visit their son on the same day and who in the course of things must come to terms with an infidelity in their own marriage. This situation speaks to the sacredness and enduring power of the institution of marriage, and in a subtle way, adds power to the main storyline.

Use subplots to add texture, contrast, and tension against your main storyline. Think of a piece of music. If your main plot is the melody, your subplots should harmonize with it. They will add flavor and visual diversity, too. Some screenplay theorists believe that the subplot is where the theme arises, and this might be true for your story, too.

But since we are writing a script from a theme-based approach, and are working towards having every aspect of the film resonate with theme, your subplots will naturally evoke your film's main idea, in a way that complements the main storyline like the perfect accessory.

Try This!

Go back to your story spine chart. Think about how minor characters in the story of your life can be developed with subplots of their own. Draw a new branch or two on the chart, tracing the arc of a lesser character or situation that somehow harmonizes with the main plotline.

Keep developing this idea for a subplot as new thoughts and insights about this story layer come to you. Use your imagination to develop the characters and storyline, but be sure to keep it tightly connected and relevant to the core of your story.

CHAPTER 8:

Building the Character Arc of Your Protagonist

We've laid the groundwork with theme and story spine, as well as characters and subplot. Now it is time to focus for a while on how the protagonist grows and changes in the story. Using theme as a guide, studying the plot, and charting growth on the page will all help you build a strong character arc that will make your story unforgettable.

There are several approaches to identifying and developing the character arc of the protagonist. The first is to use theme as a guide. Using the theme, you can examine how it is interlinked with character. This is because usually a character's journey, or narrative arc, is inherent in the theme itself. For instance, if a story's theme is that honesty is not always the best policy, then in all likelihood the main character will learn that lesson in the course of their story.

Another approach is to focus on the plotting and trace the action of the story, as it pertains to the character and their growth. This means you identify what happens, then what happens next and then ask, how does that affect the character? What new skills does he or she gain in having accomplished that goal, or experienced that situation? You can do this work on your story spine chart, or start a new chart that focuses solely on character growth.

The most important question is, how will the character grow? The trick is to transform the idea of the character's growth into action, since the protagonist must always be taking action. In this way, the ideas of the theme are reflected in the character's changes and growth.

To get started, take out a sheet of paper and write the following:

My character's name is:

He or she wants:

He or she needs:

Spend some time writing out the answers to the last two questions. Give it a whole paragraph, and keep writing until some insights come up. You will find that there is an intersection, but also a disconnect between what your character wants and what they need. It is in this disconnect that the character's growth happens.

We start out pursuing the prom queen, thinking that's what we want, but we really need the friendship and loyalty of our lab partner in science class. The growth that happens is we are realizing the importance of inner beauty and that, to quote a folk wisdom/cliché, "looks aren't everything." What you get when you explore the gap between what they want and what they need is a true character reversal, also known as the main character's narrative arc.

In the film AWAKENINGS, the character of Dr. Sayer, based on the real life character Oliver Sacks, whose memoir was the basis for the film, starts out as a recluse who turns down an offer to go out for coffee from a female colleague. But in the course of experimenting with a new drug which awakens catatonic patients, he is awakened to the importance of living every moment to its fullest. In the end, although the catatonic patients revert to their previous state, Sayer has been so transformed by the experience that he invites the same woman out for coffee. This clearly shows his narrative arc, so called because, like an arc, it goes from a low point up to a high one and then back down again. He has grown and changed as a result of his experiences.

You might want to draw an actual arc on the page, and make notes along this line, charting out the character's perceptions of something, showing their change and growth. Next to these character notes, turning points in the plot can also be listed, especially if they happen at the same time as character revelations.

Keep in mind, too, that it is almost always the forces of antagonism which produce change. That which does not kill your character makes her or him stronger. In working out the character arc, focus on the conflict. It is in the unfolding of conflict between two forces that the greatest of truths are often revealed.

Since the main character must be active, they are the ones who must have a goal within the confines of the story, and who must take action to overcome it. When obstacles are thrown in their way, and in any good drama they will be, the protagonist has to figure out how to overcome those obstacles. They must leap the hurdles, dodge the bullets, and pass all the tests that the story provides. In the course of facing all of these challenges, this main character grows and changes, and this is what ultimately creates the narrative arc.

In a dramatic story, the three acts build up to the final test at the climax. The growth and change of the main character throughout the story up to that point will strengthen him or her so that they are able to take the final challenge. In the end, as the story resolves, it becomes clear that this main character has become a different person as a result of all of their trials. The difference between who they were when they started and who they end up to be is the essence of their character arc.

Try This!

Take out a new sheet of 11x14 paper and turn it lengthwise. Draw a new line, in the same shape as the story spine arc. Use this line to chart the growth of your character. Describe his or her emotional state at the beginning of the story and try to trace and articulate the changes in his behavior, philosophy, attitudes, etc. all the way through the story, to the end of the line.

Note the places where a particular scene filled with conflict pushes him towards that growth and change. Stay conscious of how interdependent your plot and your character truly are.

CHAPTER 9:

Inventing a Frame to Propel the Story Forward

Your next task is to think about and begin inventing a frame to heighten momentum and contain the drama. A classic example of a framing device is the ticking bomb. If we see a bomb that is set to go off in an early scene, we know that the main character, and the whole story, is now under pressure to find and defuse the bomb. Similarly, a murder in the opening scene sets up a whodunit frame for the story, while a visual of a gun in someone's hand sets up the expectation that someone will get shot. But you don't need an actual bomb, murder, or gun in the bad guy's hand to have an effective frame. All it comes down to is the issue of stakes – establishing high stakes in your story early on is the key to creating story momentum and a sense of narrative urgency.

Ideally, the story frame is in sync with your theme. It needs to somehow resonate with and be reflective of your story's main idea, so that the finished screenplay has unity and power. Real life doesn't always come wrapped neatly in a three-act structure, so a frame must often be invented to impose that structure onto true events. Think of real life as your clay and the frame as the mold which will give it shape. It gives you a direction, a focus and a hook to hang your story on.

How does the frame get invented? It is born out of the themes and character traits that are apparent in the basic story. Like plot and character, it stems organically from the controlling idea. Unlike plot and character, however, the frame is much more subtle and tricky to invent. Probably the best way to figure out your frame is to study other films and see how it's done.

The film ADAPTATION is an extreme example of frame creation and is a great case study on the subject. Based on the non-fiction book *The Orchid Thief* by Susan Orlean, the film tells the story of a screenwriter's futile attempts to adapt the true story, which lacks a dramatic narrative. This serves as a frame through which the original, real-life story of orchid poachers in South Florida can be told. Another entertaining example is Tim Burton's BIG FISH, which also uses the concept of storytelling to tell the story of a dying father leaving his legacy to his son.

CATCH YOUR STORY IF YOU CAN

You may also want to take a look at the 2002 film CATCH ME IF YOU CAN, directed by Steven Spielberg and starring Leonard DiCaprio as a young genius con man and Tom Hanks as the FBI agent in charge of catching him. You'll be impressed with screenwriter Jeff Nathanson's expert manipulation of the facts in order to create sheer entertainment.

The story of Frank Abagnale, Jr., who cons Pan Am airlines out of 2.8 million with fraudulent check use, and impersonates both a doctor and a lawyer before he's even turned 19, is inherently dramatic. But no matter how amazing the facts are, a compelling film story demands a shape that keeps the audience gripping their seats in anticipation. So the writer created a very "catchy" frame to help unravel the narrative. In CATCH ME IF YOU CAN, Nathanson uses scenes from the end of Abagnale's fraud career to frame the main story of Frank's early years and progression into and through the life of crime.

In the framing scenes, which open the movie, but actually take place at the end of the crime spree story, FBI agent Hanratty (Hanks) and Abagnale (DiCaprio) are clearly friends. Even though Frank is Hanratty's captive, there is a bond between them, a sense of trust and partnership. By molding the script this way, the writer keeps us wondering how this happened. First we see them as friends, then we see them in a cat and mouse relationship. There's a disconnect, a gap. As an audience, we need to fill that gap, and answer the dramatic question of how this respect and trust was built between these two. We stay compelled through Frank's story not just because it is entertaining, but also because we need the question of how this came to be answered.

In AMELIA, the frame is Amelia's last and fatal flight around the world. This sets the tone for all else and raises the dramatic question which pulls us along through the story: How will she get there? Not just how will she get around the world, but how, in her life story, will she get to the point where she can attempt to fly around the world? When you watch the film, notice how the story of her entire flying career is told through the frame of that one last flight. The story opens with her descent into the cockpit for the trip around the world. Then, we go back to the beginning. Throughout the story, we flash forward to view parts of the trip which inform her character and help develop her themes. And then in the third act, the main storyline meets up with the frame, and the film finishes with a continuance of her journey up to her death.

A frame is a device that usually uses time cuts to give us some perspective on the real story. Although all the events portrayed in both the main story and the frame can be true, the existence of the frame helps the writer to fictionalize it, to enhance the dramatic elements, and create an artificial dose of suspense, tension and conflict. A frame does not always have to be time-based; it can instead play with space, by intercutting scenes of a subplot which happen at the same time, but somewhere else, and raise questions about the main plot. Think of SILENCE OF THE LAMBS, and how the crosscuts to the torture chamber inform Agent Starling's quest to find the culprit.

I was once hired to write a screenplay based on a woman's life whose step-father was a military spy. In my search for a frame, I decided to use the image of an old trunk, filled with documents, keepsakes and mementos. The trunk appears in the beginning of the film, which is actually the end of the story, and the woman's readiness to open the trunk takes us back to her childhood, where we see the trunk begin to be filled with things that all relate to an important mystery she needs to solve. Sometimes, starting a story towards the end and then going back to the beginning and showing us how we got there can serve as an effective frame. Whatever frame you choose, let it be organic, intuitively developed from the story.

In THE DAY SHE DROVE ME, the frame is the woman's

decision to drive her boyfriend around to all the places she's ever lived in one day. This propels the story into multiple flashbacks, which slowly reveal the reasons for her shame and fear regarding his marriage proposal.

The important thing is to use the frame you create to raise a question, by showing a disparity, or gap, in the story, which needs to be filled. The filling of that gap comes as the true story unravels in tightly paced scenes, highlighting only the most dramatic and tension-filled elements of the true story. The third act, ideally, provides a confluence of the main story and the frame, wherein the answer to the questions raised by the frame is revealed, making for a satisfying resolution to the screenplay.

When you create a frame for your story, just make sure that it raises a question in the audience's mind and propels the story forward.

A story frame can be anything. It can be someone looking back in order to solve a story question, it can be a decision that someone needs to make, or something that someone needs to prove. It can be a decision about someone's future, a judgment that needs to be made, or a task that needs to be accomplished. Tap into your imagination and see where the possibilities take you.

Try This!

Read through your message statement again. Now take thirty minutes and brainstorm ten different ideas for a frame, some story device that will propel your character through the story under pressure, with a sense of time running out or some other high-stakes motivator.

The frame should pose a dramatic question. In the course of trying to answer the question, the autobiographical material of your life, or the biographical story of someone else's, will be revealed, unfolding organically.

When you are done brainstorming, circle or underline those ideas which are most germane to your theme, and which resonate with it the most clearly.

CHAPTER 10:

Imagining the Truth to Create New Scenes

Someone once said that real life makes bad drama, and in some sense, this is true. The episodes, situations and events of our real lives, while seemingly dramatic to us, don't ever happen in a way that would be effective as entertainment on the big screen. A movie ticket these days costs close to ten dollars. But more importantly, your audience wants to be mesmerized and enchanted. They want to be carried away from their everyday reality. In order to do this, the work of telling a true story often involves at least some amount of making things up.

So instead of writing a scene that depicts one's actual memory of what happened, the dramatic scene has to be imagined, taking the truth and tweaking it with a heightened sense of conflict. How do we do this? By letting go of our literal memories just enough to allow imagination to infuse the facts with metaphor. Rather than trying to sit down and write the scene exactly as it happened, you can instead conjure up the memory and re-tell it, freeing yourself from what actually happened and thinking instead about how it might have happened, and how you can express what happened in a way that others will truly "get it."

This will require a bit of playfulness on your part – it means

73

letting loose and opening up. Let yourself go. Try not to worry about being outrageous or deceptive. Mostly, try not to worry about what really happened.

You'll find that once you start writing a scene from memory, your imagination takes over. In truth, no one really knows how much of our memory is actually imagined. What we store is so selective, and informed by so many other things, such as our emotions at the time, our desires, and our fears, that how we remember something is really not a factual representation of what happened anyway.

So, with this in mind, allow the writing process to guide you on a journey, where you retell the essence of your history, capturing the emotional truth, without necessarily adhering to the literal. Robert McKee says, "A story must be like life, but not so verbatim that it has no depth or meaning beyond what is obvious to everyone on the street."

Remember, too, that in a film story, time is sped up and action is compressed. Dialogue morphs the actual speech into a more concise and subtle form. This leads to making things up that didn't really happen in order to convey the emotional truth about what really did happen. Suddenly the line between truth and imagination blurs.

What we're talking about here is an intuitive approach to writing our scenes. Ask yourself, how can you manifest the conflict? What can you make up that will replicate and communicate your truth? You will find, also, that as much as you try to make things up and fictionalize your history, the truth will come out anyway. That's why so many great writers admit that all of their heroes are actually themselves, and all of their stories are in some way true.

Take some time and just imagine. You have a plotline, characters, a whole story. What you need now is the meat and potatoes, the actual events, alive in the scenes. Spend some time imagining the events that will take your character from point a to point b and everything in between.

SHOW, DON'T TELL

We all know that, in writing, there's nothing worse than self-indulgence. And when it comes to telling stories based on our own experience, avoiding self-pity, soap-boxing and showboating is tricky. So, just what is self-indulgent writing, and how do we avoid it in an autobiographical story? It comes down to showing instead of telling. Let the character's actions speak louder than words. Don't be preachy, overstate your point, or spell anything out. We're here to be entertained, so give us a good story. Embed your message in the far corners of the story, as subtext. Use action, dialogue, and visuals to help us stay in the moment. Take license with your story, so that it rises and falls, and keeps a brisk pace. This can often mean cutting out personal vignettes you may be attached to, but which slow the story down, or don't serve the greater good of the narrative arc.

Self-indulgence happens when we use the opportunity of having an audience to express in obvious ways how we feel. Self-indulgence also happens when we share experiences or re-tell events and stories from our past just because they have meaning to us, rather than as a result of the larger purpose and drive of the work of art we are shaping. Ask yourself, does this belong in this story? It may

75

be a valuable, important statement you want to make. It may be a traumatic or outrageous experience you want to share. But that doesn't mean you should eschew character and story development just to get your message across.

Instead, you need to step back and go in a different direction. Try to see your situation as one of many, as multi-faceted, with positives and negatives, shades of gray and nuance. Perhaps you were molested, which is of course a horrible thing. But if you have learned things about yourself and grown to develop healthy boundaries, and now help other victims, now you have turned an opportunity for self-pity into a place of acceptance. When you come from there, you write a more balanced, interesting and universal story.

It's important that you be rigorous with your writing in this area. Tread lightly on your personal views. Readers are turned off by stories that broadcast the message or try to gain sympathy for the author, without really earning true empathy through the immediacy of description, detail, action and dialogue. Let the story come alive, unfolding on its own, and notice how the personal becomes universal, enabling you to reach others much more effectively with your truth.

HIDING BEHIND FICTION

THE HELP, based on the book by Kathryn Stockett, is a fictionalized version of a true story. In the story, a wealthy white woman is trying to portray the true stories of several black women who work as maids in Jackson, Mississippi while at the same time protecting them from harm. She changes the name of the women, and the name of the town, but once her book comes out, everyone knows who it is really about. Luckily for the maids, the white ladies are so shamefully depicted in the book, they don't want to admit it is about them, so the maids have some built in protection. If only we could all have it that easy! For most of us, the concerns about exposure can be overwhelming. So much so that we can sometimes get paralyzed and lose the ability to write.

It is common practice to change the names and places to protect the innocent. But the degree to which we fictionalize depends on our own individual feelings, the feelings of others involved, and the subject matter. While some stories are too thin and plain to be told without the dressings of fiction, other stories, usually those that depict overcoming great odds (DANGEROUS MINDS) surviving disasters, (THE PERFECT STORM) or forging a great new cultural achievement (INVICTUS), call out to be presented as non-fiction. But even if we are sure that our true story would best be told as such, there are still going to be questions and hesitations, fears and anxieties about exposure and ramifications, libel and slander. How do we decide what to keep real and what to change? The best advice for this is to follow your gut. Use your instincts to tell you where to disguise the facts and where to boldly reveal them. As does everything in this schema, it comes down to your theme as well. Keep going back to your film's main idea and ask yourself if the screenplay's authenticity and integrity would be sacrificed by changing names, places, or situations. If so, then don't do it.

Sometimes, it is truly in the interest of the story and the people involved to fictionalize, even if it is just to a small degree.

Plenty of "thinly-veiled autobiography" has been well-received. Changing some names, revising some timelines, and taking liberties with locales can free you up and allow you to capture the emotional truth.

There are times when we will need to take it even further and blend truth fully with imagination, allowing the story to evolve into something new, fueled by real events, and representing some of the emotional truths of our life story, but in many ways, unabashedly made up. This is what the author of THE DEVIL WORE PRADA is said to have done. Nominated for numerous awards, the film was based upon the novel by Lauren Weisberger, and is a thinly veiled account of her time as an assistant to the editor of *Vogue* magazine. As heavily disguised as the truth was, no one could argue what the true subject matter was, since the fact that the author was an employee of *Vogue* was well known. Even with the fictionalization, there was backlash. Many influential people in the magazine world chastised the author for what they perceived as an attempt to get back at her boss for being cruel to her.

Both the novel and the film THE DEVIL WORE PRADA took huge liberties with the truth, and both eventually became blockbusters. This is a perfect example of a circumstance that calls out for fictionalization. When you are writing about people who are in the public eye, it's often best to mask the identities to protect the innocent and guilty.

SLANDER, LIBEL AND THE TRUE STORYTELLER

According to the law, defamation, which includes libel and

slander, occurs when a person or entity communicates false information that damages the reputation of another person or entity. When presenting a story as true, you can expect to be held accountable for that story's truth. If you do mutate, exaggerate, truncate, or otherwise change the facts, be sure that you're doing so in a way that will not harm the reputation of another person or entity. It's a good idea to ask a lawyer to read your autobiographical or biographical screenplay before you start sending it out, and to look closely at the script yourself, asking yourself honestly whether you have portrayed anyone or anything in a damaging manner. If so, it would behoove you to make appropriate story changes. The goal here is to make manifest a powerful, compelling work of art, not to hurt anyone, get back at someone, and certainly not to purposefully ruin anybody's life.

Maybe it's best to think about it in terms of a spectrum. On one end is the reality show or documentary, baldly capturing real events, and on the other hand, a fantasy blockbuster a la AVATAR. Both afford the audience a vicarious experience, if they're done well. But the decision as to how much we want to coat the story within us in artifice depends on both our own comfort level as well as the nature of the material. The process is intuitive, like so much of writing. We feel our way through, try different approaches, until we find the one that fits. The question of how much to fictionalize will be answered if you trust yourself, and the process of writing. Stay open to your inner wisdom, and your ideas will take the form and shape they are meant to take.

Try This!

Take thirty minutes and generate a list of ten questions that pertain to your story. Do this quickly, as a brainstorm exercise. Think in terms of who, what, why, when, and where. Pretend you are the detective on the case, trying to get to the bottom of your story.

Now, pretend you are the all-knowing entity who has all the answers. Or, better yet, pretend you are the devious criminal who is going to make up the most plausible untruths imaginable. Make the answers colorful, inventive. Avoid clichés and stereotypes at all costs. Instead, go with the unexpected answers. Above all, in this exercise, use your imagination freely, and let the ideas fly.

CHAPTER 11:

Crafting Great Dialogue From Actual Speech

The paradox of great dialogue is that it sounds so true and believable, yet is clearly not ordinary language. What makes dialogue great? How do you create sharp, witty lines? There are several important things to keep in mind when it comes to the art of getting your characters talking.

Dialogue should not be an avenue for informing the audience about motivations or story background. It should be natural and believable as something the character would say in that moment, without forcing out information the writer needs the audience to hear. Make your dialogue part of the action. In fact, it should always spring from the action, and be an organic consequence of the scene.

The trick is to design dialogue that captures the essence of real speech, yet offers a higher level of entertainment than ordinary talk. At all costs, you need to avoid being too on the nose with your dialogue. When you write a first draft, you'll often put down exactly what the character means, because you just need to get it out of your head and down on the page. Later, you will want to rewrite that dialogue so that the characters say what they don't mean.

In revision, the idea is to look at all your dialogue and make sure that it conveys meaning through subtext. When characters say the opposite of what they mean, it creates irony and subtlety. It gives the audience a more satisfying experience. Watch any great film and you will notice that the dialogue is elusive, challenging, never hitting the nail exactly on the head.

Keep asking yourself, how can this be more subtle? How can I make the audience work a little harder to read between the lines? Because that is the key to effective dialogue —the meaning must be found beneath, below, and within the superficial sound of the words.

Dialogue should also avoid stating the obvious and instead say the opposite of or an ironic twist on what the character really means. This way, the audience can "read between the lines" and enjoy the tension between what the character says and what they really mean.

Another thing to keep in mind about screen dialogue is that less is more. Cinema is an imagistic language. Dialogue should be used sparingly and as a last resort, after a visual, active image has been painted on the page which tells the story. Characters should only speak as an augment, an additional layer, on top of the action, and even then it should be sparse, leaving much to the imagination. When we do let our characters talk, every word must work hard.

Another thing to keep in mind is that dialogue needs to serve several functions in a script. First, it must somehow move the story forward, i.e. advance the plot and make something happen. Second, it must reveal character. This means that every line has to resonate with the person who says it – the flavor of their background should be captured in their word choices. The syntax, or arrangement of words, should be uniquely theirs.

For example, Harry Callahan's "Go ahead, make my day," would never be uttered by Scarlett O'Hara's maid, Prissy, in GONE WITH THE WIND, nor would Callahan ever be likely to say, "I don't know nothing 'bout birthin' babies, Miss Scarlett!" Every person has their own unique slang, attitudes and personality quirks, and these should inform the things they say as well as the way they say it. Do you see how Prissy's line not only reveals her character, but also moves the story forward? It ramps up the tension in this scene, and causes the audience to realize that Scarlett is on her own.

It also helps to think about where the character is from – East or West Coast? The South? Europe? Where exactly? What town? How do people talk from that region? Try to listen to examples until you can hear the cadence of that particular type of speech in your head. Next, think about the character as an individual. What is his or her educational background? What economic class are they in? Are they creative? Logical? Even-tempered? Emotional?

Once you have a very clear definition for this character, their dialogue will naturally come out sounding like them and only them. Keep a clear vision of your character's unique traits in mind when you draft their dialogue and especially later, when you revise and polish it. Keep hearing them talk, let them come alive in your mind, and if you're really in tune with your characters, you'll find they begin to speak through you.

Third, dialogue should always contain subtext. There is the text, and then the subtext. The words they say, and the thoughts ideas or feelings beneath those words. Without subtext, your dialogue will be too on the nose, too exact and heavy handed.

Think of Thelma and Louise at the end of their movie.

Thelma simply says, "Let's keep goin', " and Louise says, "Are you sure?" and Thelma says "Yeah." What we see is that they're at the edge of a huge cliff with the cops behind them. What we hear would mean nothing without the image. But within the context of that image, it speaks volumes. The text is the words on the surface, but the subtext is the meaning of those words, in the context of the images we see and the content of the story up to that point.

Finally, dialogue needs to evoke a visceral response and engage the audience. It needs to entertain. With only two hours of screen time, every second counts, and the writer cannot afford to leave one dull line in. Avoid clichés, stereotypes, stale jokes and dated material. Whether it's a funny line, a mysterious line, a poignant line, or a frightening one, make sure the line has some entertainment value, i.e., that it moves the audience emotionally somehow, evoking intrigue, humor, sadness, fear, or some other strong feeling in the audience.

Don't worry too much if your dialogue isn't perfect at first. A dialogue polish is often one of the last things you'll do in your work on the script. It's easier, in the later stages of revision, to feel where the dialogue is smooth and where it is still awkward. You'll be better able to identify the places where it doesn't quite do its job of conveying character, moving the story forward, suggesting subtext, and entertaining the audience, once the script is finished.

What you're going for is dialogue that rings true and speaks volumes, and that will not always come quickly or easily. But when you do create the sparkling, polished lines that all the finest actors in

84

town will want to deliver, you'll know you've done your job.

Try This!

Get your characters talking. Take two main characters and put them in an airplane together. Now have the airplane experience some sort of mechanical failure. Read what you've written out loud. Tweak any lines that feel dull. Enhance the dialogue so that it has more punch. See what you can take away, in order to add more subtext and irony.

Now, think about how you can adapt this scene or be inspired by it so that it fits into your story, which probably is not about an airplane malfunctioning. If you've generated some really good dialogue through the exercise, you can probably find a way to use it. And not only that, you can let it serve as a benchmark. Let it be the standard which the rest of your dialogue will have to live up to.

CHAPTER 12:

Putting it all Together in a Treatment

Treatments are comprehensive outlines, like blueprints, that can be used as a guideline when writing your screenplay. But they are also works of art in their own right, and should be something that a producer, agent or actor will want to lie back on his or her couch and lose themselves in for a while. Mainly, they are useful in reminding you what comes next. They are part of the process of building a story that has a three act structure, and will aid you in sharing the screenplay idea with other writers for feedback, or producers and other industry professionals to garner interest in the script. Treatments are also marketable commodities, and while it doesn't happen often, writers have been known to sell treatments without having yet written the screenplay. It is always a good idea to register a treatment with the Writers Guild of America before showing it around too much.

In the treatment, you are mostly synopsizing your story, but you also want to give snippets of dialogue, paint the texture of your story's world with descriptive prose, and fine tune and hone your structure so that it captivates your readers. Even if you don't think you'll ever show your treatment to anyone, much less use it as a marketing tool, write it for yourself, as part of the process of getting the story down.

I always find that if I write a treatment, it helps me get the screenplay written. It keeps me from getting lost, from waking up one morning and thinking, "where was I going with this again?" When I have the treatment, I can read it over and over again as I'm writing the script, and if I realize that a scene from the treatment really doesn't belong in the screenplay, I just X it out. And often times, when I'm writing the script, I'll realize that the story needs to change. The writing itself often guides us towards a deeper understanding of our story. So at that point, I might sit down and make a few changes to the treatment, always keeping it fluid, and always close at hand, to use as a guide.

A treatment is a condensed version of your story, written in present tense and in paragraph form. It will tell the story as you see it in your mind. It should be single-spaced and run about 8-15 pages using a normal, Times New Roman or Courier font in size 12. Here is an excerpt from a treatment I co-wrote with Dorothy McGrew:

SAFE WITH ME – TREATMENT

Act I

1999 – In a busy Naples, FL beauty salon, the receptionist KAY runs a tight ship. An important customer comes in. DOTTIE, 50's, is about to start on the woman's facial when she gets a call on her cell phone. She tries to ignore it, but it keeps ringing, so she decides to answer it. The busy, uptight client has a nail appointment scheduled after Dottie and reminds her that they need to stay on track. Dottie assures her it will only be a second. She picks up the phone.

Dottie doesn't recognize the voice at first. After a moment she realizes it is her brother STEVE, whom she hasn't heard from in 20 years. He's at an airport and needs her to buy him a ticket so he can fly to Naples. She can't call him back, and senses that he'll disappear again if she doesn't follow his wishes. She leaves the salon, sits outside on a bench as Steve puts her on with the airline customer service rep he's standing next to at the Las Vegas airport.

Meanwhile, the client is kept waiting, and through the glass of the shop windows, we can see her getting irate, yelling, and tension building inside the salon. Dottie tells Steve she'll see him later at the airport.

She re-enters the shop. Other stylists, including the nail tech who is supposed to take the client next, grumble, both in and out of earshot, about how their whole day is going to be thrown off now.

She explains to Kay that it was her brother. Kay has known her for ten years and didn't know she had a brother. Dottie says, "No one does."

She drives her convertible home, finds her daughter doing her homework. "Honey, I have to talk to you, there's something you should know." Her daughter is stunned to learn she has an uncle, but her friends honk the horn outside, picking her up to go see a movie. Her daughter leaves, and Dottie goes down into the basement. She pulls on a chain to light up the room with a bare bulb hanging in the ceiling. Mostly used for storage, a small sewing area. She lifts some blankets and other things off a very old, very heavy metal trunk. She sits down on the basement floor, staring at the trunk, reluctant to open it.

1959 – 40 years earlier, we are in Lincoln, Nebraska. The Mickey Mouse Club is on TV. The trunk sits against the wall in the den. Dottie, 12, watches the show. Her brother STEVE, 14, does his homework nearby. Their mother, MARGE, dances around the room during the songs, and recalls her brief stint in showbiz. She is trying to outdo the Mouseketeers, and Dot and Steve think she's silly.

Marge shows the kids a new photo album she's just finished putting together, and then puts it inside the huge, heavy trunk, which we learn is Dotty's dowry trunk. We get a glimpse of its other contents: Dotty's great grandmother's hand crocheted bed covering, her baby book and Bible, Christening dress, a handkerchief that belonged to her great grandmother, embroidered with blue flower stitching.

Nearby, on Lincoln Air Force Base, a major U.S.A.F. Strategic Air Command (SAC) bomber and missile base, navigator and bombardier BEN is applauded by his flight commander for a successful Touch 'n Go. He is teased by a co-pilot about dating an older woman with two kids and socks the guy. That evening, he shows up at Marge's and takes her and the kids out to a nice dinner.

He proposes marriage, and she accepts.

That night, Marge and Dottie discuss the marriage. We get the sense that Marge has rose-colored glasses on. She calls him her knight in shining armor, and Dot reminds her there's no such thing. "Spoilsport." Dottie gives her mom her great grandmother's handkerchief to wear as something old and something blue in the wedding.

They have a small wedding in her backyard. The question of his parents comes up. Marge tells her sister Dorothy, "They don't travel – we're going to see them for our honeymoon." Afterwards, while they're on their honeymoon, Mick and aunt Dorothy babysit the kids. Dottie, an eavesdropper, overhears a conversation in which she finds out that her mom's first husband is not really their father – that he was abusive and that her mom was having an affair. Mick is suspicious of Ben, doesn't see why he would want to marry Marge, an older woman with two kids.

On the honeymoon, they go to the Black Hills of North Dakota and he takes her to meet his parents. They have lunch out on the front porch. His mother lapses into Russian with Ben and he asks her not to, but she can't seem to help herself. That night, Marge tells Ben about her abusive first husband and admits to having a lover, who fathered her kids. She asks him to promise to keep her secret. He promises. Ben says he wants the kids to call him dad.

91

Marge and the kids move onto the base. Ben explains how things work on the base – that the officers and their families can't mix with the NCO's. All the different clubs and activities are segregated. He shows them the layout of the base housing, which is set on a hillside. The higher you go up the hill, the higher the level of brass.

Dottie learns that the stairs creak in the house one night when she is trying to eavesdrop on conversation between her mother and Ben. Ben's temper (normally cool and silent) erupts unexpectedly over Dottie's eavesdropping. Dottie now knows which of his buttons set him off. She becomes highly intense, using caution and sensing mood swings.

Happily married to her prince, Marge takes up photography. She gives Dotty a few pictures, which end up in the trunk.

Dottie tries to get Steve to go bowling, but he is too busy watching the pilots, studying their moves. Steve has put Ben on a pedestal, and wants to be a pilot just like Ben when he grows up.

We meet THE GIVINGS. Wife Jean and Marge become friends. He is a Colonel. They live on a hill above Ben and Marge. They start playing bridge, have luncheons, teas, etc. Ben is excited that Marge has been accepted by his superior's wife.

Marge has a severe asthma attack and is taken to the hospital. She thinks Ben is on a mission but when she informs the Air Force hospital staff of this, they show that he is supposed to be on base. When Ben arrives home and visits Marge in the hospital, Marge confronts him about his whereabouts. He is unsympathetic to her condition and seems more concerned that she told people he was on a mission. Kindly, subtly, he tells her he would prefer it if she didn't tell people about his whereabouts. He tries to make it seem like it's no big deal, but it makes her suspicious. From here on in, Marge's pleasant, positive attitude starts to deteriorate and she becomes increasingly self-destructive.

Steve befriends their neighbor PETE, an Air Force Lt. who is a bachelor and takes Steve under his wing, gets him into playing LaCrosse. Steve puts Pete on a pedestal and talks about him all of the time.

Ben is gone more frequently, taking longer trips. For Dottie, he always brings home costumed dolls from foreign countries such as Guam, Germany, England, France, Japan, Russia and Sweden.

Ben comes home with Staffordshire china, a Hammond organ with all the whistles, and buys a new car for Steve. "Where are you getting the money?" Dottie overhears Marge asking one night. To which Ben says, "You don't have to know everything."

She accuses him of being a spy and he implies that if she says anything about that again, he'll tell the kids who their real father is. Marge is clearly ashamed of this and doesn't want the kids to know.

End of Act I

The treatment then goes on to detail the scenes of Act II and Act III in the same manner.

Here is another example of a treatment based on a true story: http://www.scripthollywood.com/sitebuildercontent/sitebuilderfiles /blytreatment.pdf

Just as a screenplay moves from scene to scene approximately every two pages, a treatment should move from scene to scene after every paragraph of two to four sentences. Clearly introduce each new character, and give the character a short description, both physical and emotional. You don't need to capitalize the characters names as you would in a screenplay. Think of a treatment as more of a short story. It should flow and entertain, and it should be written concisely, so that every moment and every word counts. Hook your reader in from the beginning and keep us as engaged as you will in the actual script.

Some dialogue should be included, but not so much that the treatment becomes bogged down with too many full scenes. A general rule is to include one line of dialogue per scene, or paragraph. This should be formatted as one would in a short story, using quotations, dialogue tags in present tense (he says, she says) and proper fiction writing dialogue punctuation. Unlike a fiction manuscript, however, the treatment is not double spaced and the dialogue need not be in a new paragraph – instead it can be incorporated into that scene's paragraph.

Usually the treatment will convey the tone, also. Include tidbits of language that might be used in your screenplay. Paint a good picture of your settings, and try to infuse the treatment with the feeling that you want the movie of your life to have. Is this more of a comedy, suspense, drama or action film? Whatever it is, find the language, wording, bits of dialogue, and scene descriptions that will evoke a sense of the screenplay's mood and feeling.

Don't get too bogged down in the treatment. We have to stay open and let the story evolve. There's so much we don't know about our story yet. Once the actual screenwriting begins, the treatment will probably need to be revised. This is because you will get new ideas and see new connections once the characters and situations come alive on the pages in the process of dramatic writing. It then becomes an interactive process, as the screenplay informs the treatment and vice versa. You go back and change one, as it's reflected in the other. With any luck, new insights and levels will be added as you go.

A treatment can take time to create, but the benefits are huge. In a relatively short time, you create a blueprint from which to build the screenplay, a starting point for discussion and story development, as well as a possible marketing tool for interested producers.

Try This!

First, quickly lay down a "beat sheet," making a list of all the scenes you can think of and putting them in the best possible order.

Next, review the beat sheet and fill in the blanks, making sure there are no major holes in the story and that it builds from introduction, through development, to resolution. Use your story spine chart as a guide.

Finally, take each "beat" and expand upon it, cleaning it up so it is readable and feels more like a story. In each paragraph, describe a setting, name the characters, and synopsize the main, essential action of the scene. Include a snippet of dialogue that helps emphasize the point of the scene to add concrete substance. Keep working on it, until it evolves into a fully developed, fleshed out document.

CHAPTER 13:

Finding Inspiration and Conjuring up the Magic

Throughout history, creative people of all kinds have found a connection between their work and their spiritual lives. To write a great screenplay based on a true story, we need to lose ourselves and find the flow. You may think you have to wait to be hit with inspiration. But there are ways you can open up the pathways to the subconscious, where generative, idea-making originates, and poetic and abstract thought occurs.

The mind is inherently creative – the trick is tapping into that creativity on a schedule. If there is only an hour or two in the day before or after work that you have to write, you need to somehow light the fire of inspiration on demand. Since we're writing a story that is based on some of our deepest feelings and our most intense experiences, we also have to deal with the emotional resistance that might come up when it's time to sit down to the computer and actually write it.

The most important thing to remember when it comes to actually drafting your screenplay is to do it on faith. Starting is the hardest part. Making the time, sitting down at the desk, getting ready, all of these things we can do. But the actual writing is another thing altogether. What's needed is to trust in the process, let go of our fears and urges to control.

Just jump in and write something. Allow the writing process itself, and the wisdom of your subconscious, which has already generated the seeds of this story, to take over.

Remember, the story is already there. Somewhere deep down, just out of reach of your conscious mind, the perfect, whole and complete story already exists. Your job is simply to be the instrument of your unconscious, allowing your story and its lessons to emerge organically through the ongoing process of writing.

How do you get into the zone? Exercise, listening to music, free-writing, brainstorming, re-reading yesterday's pages, all of these can really help us get the creative juices flowing. Give yourself little assignments, and break it down into bite-sized pieces. You'll be amazed at what you can come up with by making a list for ten minutes.

A certain amount of letting go is necessary in order to lose yourself and allow inspiration to lead the way. It can be a struggle to turn off the logical side of ourselves, and turn on the creative switch that allows the words to flow on the page. What's important is to find a way to conjure up the magic, so you can optimize your time at the keyboard. In all these things, the idea is to allow the process of writing to show you the way, rather than trying to know the way before you write.

There are many different kinds of writers – some write fast, some write slowly. Some write early, some write late. Some write easily, and others have a more difficult time. While there are some very reliable techniques that can be used to conjure up the magic and find inspiration at the drop of a hat, some trial and error will be needed to find what works for you. Whereas one person might find that their creativity is stimulated driving a car, another might find that taking a long shower gives them new ideas.

Here are a few strategies that many writers find effective for stimulating the right brain, where creativity is housed. These will help you get in the zone quickly enough that you should be able to type out several new scenes per hour.

BREAK A SWEAT

Taking a walk, a run, swimming or working out is a very effective way to get in the zone. After about 30 minutes, consciousness starts to shift and the business and relationship obligations of life melt away, leaving more space in your mind for creative work. Try to take the work along with you (mentally) into an exercise session, and use that time to mull a story or article idea over, allowing solutions to present themselves. It is amazing how many pieces of a story puzzle can be put together, snippets of good dialogue found, and visuals imagined while working up a sweat. Some people swear by taking a shower, doing the dishes, or taking a drive. The idea is the same, whether you're "jogging" or not, you're using kinesthetic activities to "jog" your brain into an alpha state.

SET THE MOOD WITH MUSIC

The rhythm and harmony of good music can be especially beneficial for keeping the fingers typing and the words flowing. Instrumental music is often preferred because there are no lyrics to distract you from the words in your mind. Classical music of all kinds can help you relax and focus. The beat works as a motivator as well as a regulator of sentence structure, and can enhance the poetic elements of your prose and dialogue. An added bonus is that the music can mask other sounds in the environment which might be distracting.

As you move into the editing and polishing phases, play your theme music as you work. Let go, and lose yourself in the quality and energy of your chosen songs, and then notice how it affects your prose and dialogue, giving it a more artistic and flowing sheen. Let the beat help your prose become more rhythmic. Let the melodies help you express the ups and downs of the life story you're writing. Then let the notes uplift your thoughts and ideas, inspiring you to put the very best words on the page.

TRY FREE WRITING

When you're stuck on a story problem or scene development, or just can't get going at the beginning of a writing session, the solution is usually to just write as fast and as freely as possible. The key is to write recklessly, throwing words down on the page however they come out, without any attention to spelling or grammar, and definitely not worrying about whether it's good or not. The irony is that this writing, written as if it will never be seen by anyone, often produces diamonds in the rough. Writing fast, without self-criticism or inner editing, can be a powerful way to get something not just written, but written well. This is because writing quickly, keeping the fingers moving in such a way that whatever comes to mind gets put down on the page, actually opens up the line to the place of higher consciousness where brilliant solutions and highly imaginative details come from.

BE AN EARLY BIRD

Another way to access the subconscious is to get up earlier than usual and do some writing as soon as possible. The closer you are to the dream state, the more access your mind has to that irrational, yet imaginative place. It makes sense that the dreams of sleep can fuel the dreaming up of a story and screenplay.

WRITE EVERY DAY

Keeping a regular writing time and doing it every day is another way to tap into inspiration. When you tackle the screenplay every day, a little bit at a time, it is stored in the back of the mind, so that later, while going about other business, the subconscious keeps working on it. When the next writing session begins, surprises, solutions, and creative ideas just come to mind, because your whole self has become fully immersed in the project.

Try This!

For the next week, try out the various suggestions above in this chapter. Write down what works best, and jot down any other ideas you have about how to infuse your writing time with energy and inspiration.

Every day, carve out your writing time and build in some preparation time. Don't expect yourself to just dive right in. Find ways to shake off the thoughts and stressors of your everyday life and alter your consciousness a bit. You need to lose yourself in your writing, so that you can find yourself in newly imagined ways and moments of inspiration.

Chapter 14:

Getting it all Down in a First Draft

Let's face it, writing a script is hard. But if you break it down by setting goals for daily page counts, or hours you will sit at the computer, you can enjoy the process and feel a sense of accomplishment every step of the way. Because you are writing about your own life or someone else's, you have a special, human connection to the material. Because you've spent the time to develop the theme, you can now become an instrument whose sole purpose is to convey that theme through dramatic and cinematic "play" on the page.

THE TURTLE VS. THE HARE

Are you a turtle or a hare? In my work with writers over the years, I've found that there are two kinds. I call them the turtles and the hares.

The turtles are perfectionists. They can't get to page two until page one is totally complete and spectacular in every way. When their draft is (finally) done, it barely needs editing. But the problem with turtles is that sometimes they never finish a draft, because they're too concerned with making it perfect before they can move on. What they may not realize is that often you can't get something just right

103

until you've gotten all the way to the end, and gained perspective on the whole. Besides, it can take a turtle up to a decade to finish a project. What if a producer wants to see a draft in the next six months? How does a "turtle" keep from panicking? Simply put, the turtle needs to let go a little. If you are a perfectionist, you need to unclench those jaws and face the facts: the script won't be even close to perfect until you've finished the draft and then gone back and revised.

What the turtles don't know is that they might not even be able to see how to make the script perfect until after they've typed FADE OUT on an imperfect draft. Because usually, you need to see the whole before you can know how to tweak all of its parts.

The hares, on the other hand, are looser and freer in their writing style, and they will often finish a draft quickly. Their problem is that once they've finished, sometimes it's such a mess, they don't know to clean it up, or they are overwhelmed by how much fixing there is to do. For these types of writers, the dumpers who have seven different projects in the drawer they still need to work on, my advice is to roll up your sleeves and get used to being in revision mode. Sure, generating a draft can be fun, a wild ride, full of surprises and inspiration and moments of brilliance. But until you've done the hard work of rewriting, you're just not done. We'll address revising in the next chapter, but for now, let's think about how to get that first draft written.

Neither style is better than the other. It's just a function of who you are, and you can't really change that. But there are ways to avoid the pitfalls inherent in each style and to capitalize on the best, most useful aspects of that style.

First, let go of the idea that it has to be perfect. If you're afraid you'll forget the ideas you have for improving something, keep notes. You'll remember them when you need to, trust me, and your ideas will be even better and more achievable after you've gotten to the end, when you can come back with the greater perspective of seeing the whole.

And if you're the type who writes fast drafts and ends up with ten scripts in a drawer that aren't ready and may never be, it's important to have a plan. Before you start, make sure your outline or treatment is solid and well thought out. As you write, the story will change, so keep returning to your treatment and tweaking it, incorporating the changes the story is taking as it comes alive on the page, allowing the story to live and breathe, yet managing it at the same time, keeping sight of the forest, making sure the big picture, the overall story is still whole, complete, unified, and makes sense.

Whether you're a turtle or a hare, let the treatment be your guide to the script you are writing, but remember you aren't married to it, and allow the script itself, as you write it, to be a process of discovery.

Then, take those discoveries and let them inform an ongoing revision of your treatment. This way you won't get too far off track, and when it's done, the revisions will be manageable.

As discussed in the last chapter, letting go of all the logistics of our busy lives is not always easy, so you need to do everything you can to switch gears at the beginning of your writing time.

At the outset, you want to get a visual icon of the person or situation, a representation of your true story, and place it near where you work. This can be a picture or object, souvenir or memoir. Focus on that image every day as you begin to write, and let it inspire you with imaginative, dramatic angles on your subject matter.

If you need help with script formatting, there are numerous programs you can buy that will not only explain and demonstrate it all for you, but give you shortcuts and do the formatting for you. The two industry standards these days are Final Draft (www.finaldraft.com) and Movie Magic Screenwriter (www.screenplay.com)

What's important is to find the right balance between your inner turtle and your inner hare, and the most effective inspiration methods, in order to optimize your time at the keyboard. In all these things, the idea is to let the process of writing show you the way, rather than trying to know the way before you write. Trust the process and allow the magic to happen.

<u>Try This!</u>

Ready, set, go…Write the first draft. What you're going to do is write a fast discovery draft. See if you can get it all down in two months, beginning, middle and end. A screenplay is 120 pages, so that's two pages a day for two months. If it takes three months, that's okay, too. Just lay down a foot print, as fast as you can, writing from the subconscious. Try to work on it in the early mornings, or after exercise, to tap into the most creative part of the brain. Shape the clay. Understand that this is just the beginning. Just an overview, a draft. It will be rough, full of holes and typos, but we call it a discovery draft because it's an opportunity to discover what you are writing.

Don't forget to use your treatment as a guide, and if you find the story changing, tweak your treatment accordingly. Later, you can keep whatever you like, and lose all the junk. For now, just be in the process, and let the process of writing show you the way, rather than trying to know the way before you write.

CHAPTER 15:

Taking it the Extra Mile in Revisions and Beyond

You've done it. You've generated a script about your life. It tells the story of something that happened to you, but it isn't your exact story. It's everyone's now – extremely personal, and yet universal. Excellent work! Now, it's time to take the draft and fine tune it. You're going to make the switch from the right brain (creative) to the left (logical.) Making this switch is fundamental to the revision process, and several simple techniques can help you do it.

You'll find that the revision process is a different kind of writing than the generative process of getting a draft down on the page. You felt the fire-hot excitement of creativity when you were writing the story. The ideas flowed, and the words surprised even you as they appeared on the page.

The process of revision is a much different feeling, sometimes more challenging, and sometimes a little more tedious, but it can be just as satisfying. Whereas you might have had to get a little out of control to write the script, now you get to flex that control muscle and think, think, think. You're going to need to be analytical about yourself and about your writing. We're going to have to filter through what is meaningful to you, and what will be meaningful to many others. To do this, you have to get in the audience's head, trying to see your life experience, your lessons learned, and your story itself from their perspective.

To shift from the creative mode to the editorial perspective, it's important to get some distance from the material. You need to produce a shift in consciousness that gives clarity on the weaknesses and hopefully, some ideas about how to fix them.

The question is, how to give yourself "fresh eyes"? There's no better way to get an objective opinion on a script than having someone else read it. But it's usually a good idea for you to do some revising yourself before giving it to a friend, colleague, or story analyst for feedback. So how do we achieve enough of a shift in consciousness to give ourselves constructive criticism? How do we shift gears and put on our editorial cap?

It's always a good idea to take a few days, or even weeks, off. This is a great time to think about a new project and start writing it. After a break, it's time to print out the pages of your script. If you can do this in a different font, different size, or even using a different color ink than what you drafted the script in, it will help you get a sense of "fresh eyes." Try goldenrod paper instead of white, or Arial font instead of Courier. This can really help you see the script differently, both literally and figuratively.

Next, take your script pages (hard copy is a must – not environmentally-friendly, but it's much, much easier and more effective to do at least one revision on hard copy) and a favorite pen and go somewhere different from your regular writing space. If you usually write at a desk at home, then try a coffee shop. If you usually go to a library, try writing in your living room. If you write upstairs, try downstairs. If you write inside, go outside, and vice versa. Whatever it is, some change of locale, small or large, will help give you new perspective.

Primarily, as you revise, you'll focus on plot, characters and dialogue. Try to address each of these separately, in a "pass," or revision read-through, of its own. It's always best to work on one layer at a time, if for no other reason than to keep it all straight in your mind. This means that, for example, one week you will work only on the plot, and the next on the characters, then moving on to dialogue and afterward concentrating only on the pacing.

Character development is a fundamental part of any good rewrite. The lead roles and supporting roles all need to be scrutinized for dimensionality, consistency, likeability, and entertainment value. Remember that the main characters need to have a story arc, and they each need to have unique and memorable qualities.

The narrative structure also needs attention. Does it stay focused? Does it follow a three-act structure? Can you feel the drama build? There needs to be set up, development, and payoff in each scene, each act, and the script overall.

Does it deliver the pleasures of the genre? Watch several films in your script's genre or genres and see if you can't learn from them and gain a few nuggets of inspiration with which to tweak and enhance your screenplay.

Read your dialogue OUT LOUD to yourself, so you can really hear it. This will help you make changes to enhance its authenticity and flow. Remember that dialogue should evoke the unique personality of each character, move the story forward, and entertain us with subtext and irony.

Your prose needs to be sparse, yet evocative. Editing the action in a scene means paring down the description to make every word count. As Strunk and White dictate in their book, *Elements of Style*, "Omit needless words!" At the same time, the screenplay must be filled with images and be visually descriptive enough for a reader to see the unique world being painted. Writing that stimulates the five senses is always richer.

Each of these building blocks contributes towards the whole health of the story. Without attention to all of them, your script will probably have weaknesses and likely be passed over by an industry executive.

Once you've revised the script with attention to the above elements, let it sit again for a bit. Then pick it up and examine it for the following, as you continue to fine-tune your dramatic masterpiece:

- o Scenes must be concise. The rule is to get in, accomplish the goal of the scene and get out, by cutting to the next scene.
- o End the scene on a question, leaving the audience hanging.
- o Use variety in your pacing to keep audience interest strong. Alternate fast scenes with slow ones, happy scenes with sad ones, and longer scenes with short ones.
- o Each scene needs to contain conflict. This is defined as two or more opposing forces going up against each other. Someone wants something, but someone or something is getting in their way. How will they overcome obstacles to get

it?

To be well-written, a script needs a lengthy revision process, since there are so many different elements that need to be shaped and developed. How long will you take? As long as it takes. Give yourself several months, at least. Be patient, and stick with it.

My general rule of thumb is that when you are positive that you are totally done, can't stand looking at it anymore or thinking about it, and feel compelled to send it off to everyone you know, you're not done yet. Keep working on it.

On the other hand, when you're sure it will never be done, can't stop working on it, and are afraid to send it to anyone for fear they'll hate it, you probably ARE done. At least for now. At that point, find trusted readers, one, two or three, outside your family, and ask them to read it. Let them know it's just a draft. Heave a big sigh of relief and let it be out of your hands for a while.

"The time to begin writing...is when you have finished it to your satisfaction," Mark Twain once wrote. His words apply to all writers. Every time you go through the script and work on an element, you are one step closer to having a compelling, original screenplay, written from deep within yourself.

This is the screenplay no one else could have written, and that is what will give it the power to move and entertain the masses. It began with you, and the story deep within you, but now it has evolved into something much larger. Now it has the potential to reach people and to be something they may never forget.

Try This!

Revision happens in two strokes: first the forest, then the trees. First, you put your pen away and read through the whole script without making a mark. This is the time to just smoothly give it one long read. Then sit down and make a bunch of notes and comments on the pages. Try pretending you are someone else, an actor or studio executive, perhaps, while reading these pages and making the notes.

Find the script's strengths and weaknesses. Note as many suggestions for improvement as you can think of. Once all the notes are done, it's time to make the changes. Remember, it's a process. Breaking the revision down into elements, and rewriting one element at a time is the key to a producing a much improved new draft.

Keep going until you know undeniably that you have created something great, and that it is ready to be shared.

Recommended Reading

Story: Substance, Structure, Style and the Principles of Screenwriting by Robert McKee

Your Life as Story by Tristine Rainer

The Hero with a Thousand Faces by Joseph Campbell

Aristotle's Poetics with an introductory essay by Francis Fergusson

Aristotle's Poetics for Screenwriters by Michael Tierno

The Art of Dramatic Writing by Lajos Egri

Screenplay by Syd Field

The Screenwriter's Bible by David Trottier

Recommended Viewing: Films Based on Actual Events

Often, the most valuable lessons can be gleaned from watching films based on true stories and seeing how it's done. Watch as many as you can, and watch consciously, with an eye and an ear toward structure, characterization and dialogue. Take notes. As you analyze the films, try to identify how theme helps shape their story.

- Battleship Potemkin (1925)
- The General (1927)
- Napoléon (1927)
- Cleopatra (1934)
- Mutiny on the Bounty (1935)
- Edison, The Man (1940)
- The Pride of the Yankees (1942)
- Moulin Rouge (1952)
- Houdini (1953)
- Titanic (1953)
- Lust for Life (1956)
- The Wrong Man (1956)
- A Night to Remember (1958)
- Spartacus (1960)
- Judgment at Nuremberg (1961)
- Birdman of Alcatraz (1962)

117

- The Miracle Worker (1962)
- Mutiny on the Bounty (1962)
- Lawrence of Arabia (1962)
- The Sound of Music (1965)
- Bonnie and Clyde (1967)
- In Cold Blood (1967)
- Butch Cassidy and the Sundance Kid (1969)
- Patton (1970)
- Brian's Song (1971)
- The French Connection (1971)
- Nicholas and Alexandra (1971)
- Lady Sings the Blues (1972)
- Serpico (1973)
- Dog Day Afternoon (1975)
- All the President's Men (1976)
- Bound For Glory (1976)
- Helter Skelter (1976)
- MacArthur (1977)
- The Buddy Holly Story (1978)
- Midnight Express (1978)
- Escape From Alcatraz (1979)
- Norma Rae (1979)
- Breaker Morant (1980)
- Coal Miner's Daughter (1980)
- The Elephant Man (1980)
- Raging Bull (1980)
- Mommie Dearest (1981)

- Gandhi (1982)
- Cross Creek (1983)
- Frances (1983)
- Silkwood (1983)
- The Right Stuff (1983)
- Amadeus (1984)
- The Killing Fields (1984)
- Out of Africa (1985)
- The Falcon and the Snowman (1985)
- At Close Range (1986)
- Heartburn (1986)
- Hoosiers (1986)
- The Mission (1986)
- Cry Freedom (1987)
- La Bamba (1987)
- The Last Emperor (1987)
- Matewan (1987)
- Salvador (1986)
- The Untouchables (1987)
- The Accused (1988)
- Bird (1988)
- A Cry in the Dark (1988)
- Eight Men Out (1988)
- Mississippi Burning (1988)
- Talk Radio (1988)
- Tucker: The Man and His Dream (1988)
- Glory (1989)

- My Left Foot (1989)
- Born On The Fourth Of July (1989)
- Awakenings (1990)
- Europa Europa (1990)
- GoodFellas (1990)
- Not Without My Daughter (1990)
- Bugsy (1991)
- JFK (1991)
- And the Band Played On (1993)
- Gettysburg (1993)
- Rudy (1993)
- Schindler's List (1993)
- Cool Runnings (1993)
- Ed Wood (1994)
- Heavenly Creatures (1994)
- The Madness of King George (1994)
- Mrs. Parker and the Vicious Circle (1994)
- Quiz Show (1994)
- Apollo 13 (1995)
- Braveheart (1995)
- Casino (1995)
- Dangerous Minds (1995)
- Nixon (1995)
- Bastard Out of Carolina (1996)
- The Ghost and the Darkness (1996)
- Michael Collins (1996)
- Seven Years In Tibet (1997)

- Amistad (1997)
- Boogie Nights (1997)
- Donnie Brasco (1997)
- Prefontaine (1997)
- Private Parts (1997)
- Titanic (1997)
- Gods and Monsters (1998)
- Patch Adams (1998)
- Saving Private Ryan (1998)
- Boys Don't Cry (1999)
- Girl, Interrupted (1999)
- The Messenger: The Story of Joan of Arc (1999)
- October Sky (1999)
- Thirteen Days (2000)
- Almost Famous (2000)
- Erin Brockovich (2000)
- The Perfect Storm (2000)
- A Beautiful Mind (2001)
- Black Hawk Down (2001)
- Blow (2001)
- Riding in Cars with Boys (2001)
- Catch Me If You Can (2002)
- 8 Mile (2002)
- Chicago (2002)
- Dahmer (2002)
- Frida (2002)
- The Laramie Project (2002)

- The Pianist (2002)
- Bloody Sunday (2002)
- Antwone Fisher (2003)
- Monster (2003)
- Seabiscuit (2003)
- The Aviator (2004)
- Friday Night Lights (2004)
- Beyond the Sea (2004)
- Hotel Rwanda (2004)
- Ray (2004)
- Finding Neverland (2004)
- The Motorcycle Diaries (2004)
- Capote (2005)
- Cinderella Man (2005)
- Marley & Me (2008)
- Lords of Dogtown (2005)
- Syriana (2005)
- Walk the Line (2005)
- The World's Fastest Indian (2005)
- Coach Carter (2005)
- The Zodiac (2006)
- Gridiron Gang (2006)
- Glory Road (2006)
- The Pursuit of Happyness (2006)
- The Queen (2006)
- United 93 (2006)
- American Gangster (2007)

- Becoming Jane (2007)
- Charlie Wilson's War (2007)
- Freedom Writers (2007)
- I'm Not There (2007)
- Into the Wild (2007)
- Sybil (2007)
- 21 (2008)
- Changeling (2008)
- Che (2008)
- The Duchess (2008)
- Frost/Nixon (2008)
- Milk (2008)
- The Other Boleyn Girl (2008)
- Valkyrie (2008)
- W. (2008)
- The Blind Side (2009)
- Julie & Julia (2009)
- Notorious (2009)
- Amelia (2009)
- Invictus (2009)
- The Informant! (2009)
- Hachiko: A Dog's Story (2009)
- The Social Network (2010)
- 127 Hours
- The Fighter (2010)
- Secretariat (2010)
- The King's Speech (2010)

About the Author

Candace Kearns Read has worked for twenty years in the film industry as a story analyst, screenwriter and screenwriting instructor, many of those years in the demanding and high stakes world of talent and literary agencies. Read began her career as a story analyst for The William Morris Agency and International Creative Management. The clients she has read scripts for include Michelle Pfeiffer, Denzel Washington, Anthony Hopkins, Marlon Brando, Mel Gibson, Nicolas Cage, Roger Spottiswoode (Director, TOMORROW NEVER DIES), Jeff Woolnough (Director, THE DON CHERRY STORY and CELINE), John Wells Productions and Village Roadshow Pictures. Over the years she has worked on many films, including DANGEROUS MINDS, NIXON, WHITE OLEANDER, CRIMSON TIDE, COURAGE UNDER FIRE, TRAPPED IN PARADISE, THE EDGE, INSTINCT, MEET JOE BLACK, ISLAND OF DR. MOREAU, and many others. She has written over a dozen screenplays, all of which have been either optioned or commissioned by producers. Her scripts have been in development with Fox, Disney, Lifetime and HBO. Read teaches writing at Metropolitan State College of Denver and Antioch University, and is a script consultant to film industry professionals as well as aspiring screenwriters all over the world. She earned her BFA in Dramatic Writing from New York University and received an MFA in Creative Writing from Antioch University.

CPSIA information can be obtained
at www.ICGtesting.com
Printed in the USA
FSOW03n1117110517
34159FS